MAIN MENU

U USAGE ISSUES

U1 Pronoun Case 86
  a. *I* or *Me* 86
  b. Appositives 86
  c. *We* or *Us* 87
  d. Pronouns with *Than* or *As* 87
  e. Pronouns with Infinitives 87
  f. Pronouns with Gerunds and Present Participles 88
  g. Pronouns as Subject Complements 88
U2 Pronoun Choice 88
  a. *Who* or *Whom* 88
  b. *That* or *Which* 89
U3 Inclusive Language 89
  a. Ethnicity and Race 89
  b. Gender 89
U4 Comparatives and Superlatives 91
  a. Absolute Terms 91
U5 Active and Passive Voice 91
U6 Split Infinitives 91

P PUNCTUATION

P1 The Comma 94
  a. Commas to Separate 94
  b. Commas to Set Off 94
  c. Misuses of the Comma 96
P2 The Semicolon 97
P3 The Colon 97
P4 Quotation Marks 99
  a. Direct Speech 99
  b. Short and Long Quotations 99
  c. Titles 100
  d. Other Uses for Quotation Marks 101
  e. Quotation Marks with Other Punctuation 101
P5 The Apostrophe 102
  a. Possession 102
  b. Contractions 103
  c. Plurals 103
P6 The Slash 103

P7 Parentheses 104
P8 Brackets 104
P9 The Dash 105
P10 Ellipses 105

M MECHANICS

M1 Underlining or Italics 108
  a. Titles of Works 108
  b. Other Uses 108
M2 Capitalization 109
  a. Sentence Capitals 109
  b. Proper Nouns 110
M3 Abbreviations 111
  a. Titles of Persons 111
  b. Geographical Names 111
  c. Acronyms and Initialisms 112
  d. Era Designations and Time of Day 112
M4 Numbers 113
  a. Spelling Out 113
  b. Punctuation of Numbers 114
  c. Uses of Numbers 114
  d. Symbols and Units of Measurement 115
M5 Hyphens 115
  a. Compound Words 115

R RESEARCH ESSAYS

R1 Defining the Assignment 118
  a. Audience 118
  b. Purpose 118
  c. Scope 119
  d. The Instructions 119
  e. Research Requirements 120
R2 Developing a Preliminary Thesis 120
R3 Conducting Research 121
  a. Reference Books 121
  b. Electronic Catalogues 122
  c. Research and the Internet 122
  d. The Working Bibliography 122
R4 Reading 123
  a. Previewing 123
  b. Note-Taking 124
  c. Taking Stock 124

R5 Using Note Cards 124
R6 Drafting the Essay 125
  a. Outlining 126
  b. Segmenting 126
  c. Writing a Draft Introduction 126
  d. Incorporating Quotations 126
R7 Revising the Essay 128

D DOCUMENTATION

D1 Avoiding Plagiarism 131
D2 MLA Style 133
  a. Parenthetical References 133
  b. Content and Bibliographical Notes 135
  c. List of Works Cited 135
  d. MLA-Style Sample Essay 149
D3 APA Style 152
  a. Parenthetical Citations 152
  b. Content Footnotes 154
  c. List of References 155
  d. APA-Style Sample Essay 162

J JOB-RELATED WRITING

J1 Business Documents 168
  a. Memos 168
  b. Formal Letters 169
  c. Reports 176
J2 The Job Search 178
  a. Cover letters 178
  b. Résumés 180
  c. Interviews 183
J3 Developing Exam Strategies 184
  a. Before the Exam 184
  b. During the Exam 185
  c. Multiple-Choice and Short-Answer Exams 187

Index 188
Focus on ESL 196
Correction Abbreviations Inside back cover

SECOND EDITION

A

CANADIAN WRITER'S POCKET GUIDE

Jack Finnbogason
Kwantlen University College

Al Valleau
Kwantlen University College

THOMSON

NELSON

Australia   Canada   Mexico   Singapore   Spain   United Kingdom   United States

THOMSON

NELSON

A Canadian Writer's Pocket Guide,
Second Edition

by Jack Finnbogason and Al Valleau

Editorial Director and Publisher:
Evelyn Veitch

Acquisitions Editors:
Chris Carson and
Anne Williams

Marketing Manager:
Cara Yarzab

Developmental Editor:
Rebecca Rea

Production Editor:
Bob Kohlmeier

Production Coordinator:
Helen Jager Locsin

Creative Director:
Angela Cluer

Interior Design:
Ken Phipps

Proofreader:
Joan Rawlin

Cover Design:
Ken Phipps

Cover Photograph:
David Rhodes

Compositor:
Zenaida Diores

Printer:
Transcontinental Printing Inc.

COPYRIGHT © 2002 by Nelson,
a division of Thomson Canada Limited.

Printed and bound in Canada
   3   4   04   03

For more information contact Nelson,
1120 Birchmount Road, Scarborough, Ontario, M1K 5G4. Or you can visit our Internet site at http://www.nelson.com

Student essay in Section D2, on Edward Albee, by Freda Johnson. Student essay in Section D3, on Francis Galton, by Charles F. Carington-Smith. Reprinted courtesy of Charles F. Carington-Smith.

National Library of Canada Cataloguing in Publication Data

Finnbogason, Jack, 1942–
A Canadian writer's pocket guide

2nd ed.
Includes index.
ISBN 0-17-616973-3

1. English language—Rhetoric.   2. English language—Grammar.
I. Valleau, Al, 1946–
II. Title.

PE1408.F452 2002
808'.042
C2001-903351-6

FUNDAMENTALS OF WRITING

Over three thousand years ago, Greek thinkers believed that the writing process could be profitably studied by breaking it down into three stages: invention, disposition (writing and ordering), and style (manner, tone, and rhetorical strategies). The comparable stages today are *prewriting, drafting,* and *revising*. These activities are *recursive* in that writers perform them simultaneously.

F1   Prewriting I: The Basics

Typically, when you first sit down to write, it is in response to an assignment, whether it be a report, a review, a summary, or an essay. The basic questions that confront you at the beginning of a writing project are related to five main elements: *purpose, audience, stance, research*, and *outline*.

F1-a   Purpose

To write well, you have to understand your aim or intention. You need to know if you are writing to inform, persuade, describe, narrate, summarize, define, explain, recommend, or compare. The following guidelines will help you to articulate the purpose of your assignment.

- Read the instructions in the assignment carefully.
- Underline the key verbs in the assignment. (See R1-d for information about verbs you are likely to encounter in assignment instructions.)
- Ask a classmate what he or she thinks the purpose of the assignment is.
- Learn to distinguish the demands of different types of writing. For example, a *comparison* asks you to examine two or more topics to find similarities and differences; an *analysis* asks you to examine the elements or parts of a topic.
- Make a rough outline of your intended response to the assignment and ask your instructor for feedback.

F1-b   Audience

If you are writing an assignment for a class, your audience will most likely be your instructor. If you are asked to write a report that will be read by a wider audience, you need to ask yourself questions about its members. Will they be informed or unaware? hostile or sympathetic? attentive or easily distracted?

F1-c   Stance

To understand stance fully, you first have to know that your relationship to your audience creates your *voice*, and your relationship to your topic creates your *tone*. How you feel about your topic supplies your tone, while how you see your audience—and, more particularly, how you want that audience to see you—creates your voice. A writer's stance, then, is the combined effect of voice and tone. If you are certain of what your voice and tone should be, you will not have problems with stance.

F1-d   Research

One of the first questions you must answer in the prewriting stage is whether you need to conduct formal research or whether the information you already possess is adequate. For information about the research process, see R3.

F1-e   Outline

The easiest way to start building an outline is to examine the information you have gathered in the previous stages of prewriting. The sample outline that follows shows how a topic (in this case, Canadian multiculturalism) can be broken down into its constituent parts.

I. Early influences on Canadian ethnicity

    A. Development in Upper and Lower Canada

        1. New France

        2. English coastal settlements in Canada

    B. Movement west

        1. Hudson Bay Company

        2. North-West Company

        3. Red River settlement and the Métis people

    C. Late-nineteenth-century immigration patterns

        1. Northern European and Ukrainian immigration to the prairies

        2. Chinese labour in B.C. and the head tax

II. Mid-twentieth-century shifts in immigration and ethnicity [and so on through the rest of the outline]

3

Remember that an outline is a guide only; feel free to make adjustments as new ideas occur to you. For information about outlines used in research essays, see R6-a.

F2   Prewriting II: Techniques

During the prewriting stage, you can explore your topic by using one or more of the following techniques: *brainstorming, freewriting and looping, mind-mapping, branching, the pentad,* or *topic analysis.*

F2-a   Brainstorming

Brainstorming is an exercise in free association that involves listing ideas about a topic as they occur to you. As you perform this activity, do not pause to reflect on organizational considerations such as the order of the ideas and the relationships between the ideas. Simply list as quickly as possible all the ideas that come to you.

F2-b   Mind-Mapping

To create a mind-map, take a blank sheet of paper and write your topic in the centre of the page. Draw a circle around the topic. Then write down the major ideas associated with the topic, circle each idea, and draw lines connecting the ideas to the topic in the centre. Next, write down minor ideas that relate to the major ideas, circle the minor ideas, and connect them to the main ideas. If even more specific ideas occur to you, record those ideas and connect them to the minor ideas. Continue this process until you run out of ideas. A mind-map of the problems that part-time work creates for students might look like the one in Figure F-1.

F2-c   Freewriting and Looping

The freewriting process is simple. Set a time limit of five minutes or so and write continuously about the topic, never letting your pen stop. If you cannot think of any ideas, keep writing *thinking* or *can't write* until something does come to mind.

Looping is a more directed form of freewriting and an ideal method for exploring how you feel about a topic. First, produce a statement (e.g., "When I think about Louis Riel, I think . . .") and spend five minutes freewriting about that statement. Next, read what you have written and isolate one sentence, image, or phrase that surprises you the most. Use this unexpected ele-

FIGURE F-1 Mind-Map

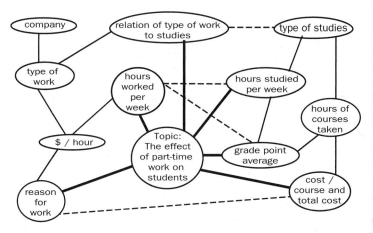

ment as your starting point for another five minutes of free-writing. Continue this process until you reach a point of diminishing returns.

F2-d Branching

Branching is a variation on mind-mapping. The chief difference is that branching proceeds in a much more linear way. The first step in branching is to break your topic down into as many parts as suggest themselves to you. If your analysis were to produce five topic parts, you would be left with five branches to explore. To the right of each branch, you would add new branches consisting of supporting ideas.

Branching gives you a better understanding of how the parts of your topic relate to one another. It also gives you a clearer sense of any gaps in your knowledge of the topic.

F2-e The Pentad[1]

The pentad is a set of five headings that helps you to discover, classify, and organize the relationships among the parts of your topic. This prewriting technique emerged in part from the work of the critic Kenneth Burke and in part from the

---

[1] Adapted from W. Ross Winterowd, ed., *Contemporary Rhetoric: A Conceptual Background with Readings* (New York: Harcourt Brace Jovanovich, 1975), 155–62.

traditional questions of journalism—*who*, *what*, *when*, *where*, *how*, and *why*. The pentad, based on Burke's five terms (listed below), is a useful mechanism for generating additional details when you are writing an essay about people and/or events.

1. Act (the *what*): the central event, what happened

2. Scene (the *when* and *where*): the background of the event, including its physical space and the time of its occurrence

3. Agent (the *who*): the person or persons involved

4. Agency (the *how*): the means by which the act or event was accomplished

5. Purpose (the *why*): the intended objective or end, the reason the act was committed or the event occurred

Listed below are the ten possible pairings (or *ratios*, as Burke calls them) you can use to explore a topic that involves actions or people.

Act – Scene	Scene – Agent	Agent – Agency	Agency – Purpose
Act – Agent	Scene – Agency	Agent – Purpose	
Act – Agency	Scene – Purpose		
Act – Purpose			

Burke's ratios allow you to examine the relationships among the main parts of your topic. For example, *Act–Purpose* forces you to answer central questions about the event and its intent, while *Act–Agent* yields useful connections between the event and the person who caused the event. By analyzing these and other ratios, you may generate additional details as well.

F2-f Topic Analysis

Called *topoi* (topics) by the Greeks, topic analysis is a prewriting technique that involves using a set list of questions to generate details about your topic. The activities associated with topic analysis (comparing, contrasting, defining, classifying, and so forth) require you to examine your topic carefully. The sample topic analysis questions that follow are adapted from a list prepared by the American rhetorician Richard Larson.[2]

---

[2] Adapted from W. Ross Winterowd, ed., *Contemporary Rhetoric: A Conceptual Background with Readings* (New York: Harcourt Brace Jovanovich, 1975), 144–54.

Exploring a single item

What are its physical characteristics? From what perspectives can it be examined? What is its structure? How are its parts put together? To what class does it belong? What uses does it have? Who uses it? Who or what produced it?

Exploring an event or process

What happened? (Be precise.) What circumstances surrounded this event or process? What were its causes? What were its consequences? Who or what was affected by it? What class of events or processes does it belong to? Is it good or bad, desirable or undesirable? By whose standards? How do you know about it? How reliable is your information? To what other events is it connected?

Writing about abstract concepts (such as socialism or capitalism)

To what items, group of items, events, or group of events does the word connect? What characteristics must an item or event have before this name can be applied to it? How do the characteristics of this item or event differ from those of other items or events included in the same class? How has the term been used by writers you have read? How have they defined it? Do you feel positive toward the item or event named by this term? Negative? What standard inclines you to feel this way?

F3 Prewriting III: Skill Development

F3-a Reading Skills

The further you get in your education, the more you shift from reading for information to critical reading. Do not accept what others have written without being critical. Use the following questions to help you become a critical reader.

- What is the writer's purpose?
- Does the writer have a concealed purpose or unannounced bias?
- What do you think the writer's key assumptions are?
- Is any pertinent information ignored?
- Does the point of view distort the material?

- Is the material current?
- Has the writer acknowledged any opposing views and dealt with them?
- Are there any logical problems with the material?
- How does what you know about the topic differ from the information the author presents?
- Does the author support his or her opinions with evidence? Is the evidence convincing? Is it current?
- Is the author an expert in the field? If not, what does he or she know about the field?
- Is the material based on *primary evidence* (the evidence of the author) or on *secondary evidence* (the evidence of others)? If the latter, are the "others" experts in the field?

Techniques such as *previewing, skimming and scanning, highlighting*, and *note-taking* provide concrete assistance as you engage in the reading process.

PREVIEWING

Before you read a book or an article, you should preview it. Previewing ranges from looking through the table of contents or index of a book to scanning the headings and illustrations of an article. Previewing helps you separate essential from nonessential information.

SKIMMING AND SCANNING

Skimming and scanning a text go hand in hand with previewing. Whereas previewing a text focuses on particular items, such as a book's index, table of contents, and headings, *skimming* lets you move through the text by reading the first sentence of a passage and quickly assessing the passage's content. You do not read every sentence when you skim a passage; you simply focus on phrases and important terms to arrive at a quick picture of what is in a passage. If you think the passage is of value, you eventually go back and read it carefully. *Scanning* a passage has the same effect. In scanning, you use your finger or a ruler to guide your eye quickly down the centre of the page. When you do this, you are not reading individual words; rather, you are gaining a quick impression of the content of each line of print.

HIGHLIGHTING

Highlighting by means of a highlighter or a pen is an effective way to show the important points in a passage. What you highlight will depend on your purpose.

Another form of highlighting is the marginal note. Marginal notes identify the main idea of each paragraph in the passage. Appended to some of the marginal notes are asterisks, which indicate the relative importance of the paragraph; the greater the number of asterisks, the greater the paragraph's importance.

NOTE-TAKING

Although most students have learned to take notes from a classroom blackboard, few have learned to take effective notes while listening to a speaker or a discussion. The same problem presents itself when students are faced with taking notes on material they have read and highlighted. When taking notes, you should consider the following factors:

1. *Are the notes connected to a text?* If so, make sure you have the author's name, the book or article title, the correct library call number, and the page number of each passage that the instructor has referred to. In addition, ask yourself the following questions:

   • Are there any definitions or facts I should record?

   • Does the material cover what I thought it would, or does it cover ground I was not expecting to cover?

   • Is there anything in the material I do not understand?

   • Do my notes cover the material?

2. *Are the notes connected to group discussions or lectures?* If so:

   • What is the topic of the discussion?

   • Am I responding to a set of discussion questions?

   • What have I highlighted as the main ideas?

   • Are there any cross-references to a text from the discussion or lecture? (If there are, note the page references.)

3. *Are the notes intended as primary work for an assignment?* If so, the topic of your assignment is the organizing factor for your notes. This type of note-taking is what you will be doing when you are asked to research outside of the course's assigned texts. For more information about the note-taking process, see R4–b.

F3-b   Listening Skills

Listening skills are as important as reading skills. Here are a few questions you can ask yourself to judge whether you are an active and critical listener:

- What is the main idea the speaker is presenting?
- Are there any supporting facts I should be taking note of?
- Can I predict what the speaker is going to say next or how he or she is going to conclude?
- Do I have any questions about the material? If so, what are they?
- Can I apply the material the speaker is presenting to other material I know?
- Is there any material I disagree with? Why do I disagree with it?

F3-c   Critical Thinking Skills

Critical thinking skills include *inference, causal analysis, summary, analysis, evaluation,* and *synthesis.*

INFERENCE

An inference is the reasoned product of two or more facts. If you know that both the Winnipeg Jets and the Quebec Nordiques were unable to survive as NHL franchises, what might you infer from these separate facts? If some members of OPEC reduce their output of oil, prices rise at the pump. What do these facts suggest in combination? Whatever you decide in response to this question will be an inference.

CAUSAL ANALYSIS

There are two key elements you need to learn. The first is the ability to discriminate among contributory, necessary, and sufficient causes. A *contributory cause*, as its name implies, is one that assists in the creation of an effect but is not sufficient by itself to produce that effect. A *necessary cause* is one that must be present if an effect is to result but is not by itself sufficient to produce that effect. A *sufficient cause* is the cause or causes that, alone or working together, will ensure that a certain effect is the result. A primary objective of causal analysis is to identify sufficient cause.

The second key element is to learn to distinguish among *immediate* causes, *intermediate* causes, and *remote* causes. These three terms refer to how close in time a cause is to an effect. You will be surprised how often a remote cause turns out to be more important than an immediate cause. The earth tremors that are part of an earthquake, for instance, are not as important to that effect as are shifting plates, a decidedly remoter cause.

SUMMARY

The simplest test of your mastery of reading is the summary. A summary tries to reduce the original prose by at least 75 percent. The length of the summary of a paragraph or a passage will vary according to whether the material is making a series of points or simply developing an elaborate illustration that needs very little summarizing. The following guidelines will help you develop a summary.

1. Read the passage. You might want to highlight or underline key points.

2. Reread the passage.

3. Find the major claim in the first paragraph of the passage and write it down. Do the same for all other paragraphs.

4. Eliminate all illustrations or examples that may appear in these paragraphs, unless an illustration is an integral part of the claim.

5. Examine any definitions that appear in the paragraphs of the passage and decide if they are important.

6. If you copy a phrase of the original passage, make sure you identify it as a quotation so that you will know to treat it as such if you subsequently use the phrase in your own work. Remember, too, that if you summarize a passage and use it in your work, you will need to give a reference for the material.

7. Once you have assembled the raw materials for your summary (claims, essential definitions, illustrations, dates, facts), use them to help you write the first draft.

8. As you write your first draft, remember to express the main points of the passage in your own words.

9. Check your first draft to see that it includes all the essential material and is written in your own words. Edit, and look for places where you can combine or condense statements.

10. Write a final draft in which you concentrate on clarity and effective sequencing.

ANALYSIS

Analyzing means "taking apart." This process involves a three-step approach.

1. Divide the topic you are analyzing into its constituent parts.

2. Study the individual parts to see what each contributes to the whole.

3. Reassemble the parts into the whole, commenting on the connections between the parts and the whole.

EVALUATION

An evaluation states why something has, or does not have, value. You have to demonstrate, as concretely as possible, some grounds that support your claim or thesis. Here are four basic steps to follow:

1. State your claim.

2. Present criteria to provide an objective test of your claim.

3. Apply the criteria carefully and thoroughly.

4. Restate your claim, but now as a proven rather than merely asserted claim.

SYNTHESIS

Synthesis is the reverse of analysis. To synthesize, you must put things together rather than take them apart. A typical synthesis involves assembling and presenting the views of three or more informed people on a particular topic. A critical synthesis requires you to do more than point out areas of agreement and disagreement among your sources; you must also indicate which view(s) you support and why.

F4 Drafting

A clear understanding of the conditions in which you write will help to smooth your progress through this challenging stage of the writing process.

F4-a Writing Preferences

Some writers are happiest writing quickly. Others tend to be more reflective and build their work slowly. It is important to understand, and work according to, your own idiosyncrasies and preferences as a writer. If you are most comfortable writing one part of your draft at a time, then do so. If you prefer to complete your first draft at a single sitting, then feel free to use that strategy.

F4-b   The Importance of Routine

You should establish a routine for drafting. Routine includes the order in which you do tasks. Whereas some writers like to begin with an easy task and thereby build confidence, others prefer to dispense with the most challenging tasks first. Ritual also has to do with where you work, when you work, and what kind of atmosphere you work in. There is no right way or wrong way to write. Establish a routine that suits you, and stick to it.

F5   Revising

Once you have completed your first draft, set it aside for a few days. When you revisit your draft, you should do so with a more critical eye. Your editing will be more effective if you focus on one facet of your draft at a time. Four editing tasks that will help you do this are the *structure sweep, the development sweep, the special-paragraphs sweep*, and the *proofreading sweep*. (For further information about these editing tasks, see R7.)

F5-a   Structure Sweep

The most efficient way to start revising your first draft is to do a structure sweep. When conducting this kind of editing sweep, ask yourself the following questions about the draft:

- Does each paragraph relate clearly to the preceding paragraph and to the following paragraph?
- Does each paragraph have a focus and a purpose?
- Does each paragraph connect to and advance my thesis?
- Is my argument balanced? Are all of its parts equally developed?

F5-b   Development Sweep

The goal of a development sweep is to verify that the ideas in your draft are supported sufficiently. Using a pen or highlighter, underline or highlight the sentences that define, illustrate, or otherwise support the main ideas you highlighted during the structure sweep. If your underlining or highlighting in a particular paragraph yields only one or two supporting sentences, that paragraph's main idea is probably not adequately supported.

F5-c   Special-Paragraphs Sweep

The focus of a special-paragraphs sweep is the introduction, the conclusion, and any other special paragraphs you have written. To begin your special-paragraphs sweep, ask yourself the following questions about the introduction:

- Does it capture the reader's attention?
- Does it clearly establish my claim (thesis)?
- Does it define difficult or challenging terms?
- Does it provide the background necessary to a successful argument?

Next, respond to the following questions about the conclusion:

- Does it restate my claim?
- Does it summarize the main points supporting my argument?
- Does it reiterate the general significance of my topic?
- Does the last sentence express an appropriate note of finality?

F5-d   Proofreading Sweep

The purpose of a proofreading sweep is to eliminate errors in usage, spelling, and punctuation. Here are some guidelines to assist you with the process:

- Read your essay aloud. Some errors or omissions become more obvious when you hear them.
- After obtaining your instructor's approval, have a fellow student proofread your essay.
- Set your draft aside for a few days and then return to it. Gaining distance from your essay generally leaves you in a better position to spot errors.
- Use past graded assignments to determine what your most common errors are. Check that they haven't reappeared in your draft.
- Check against MLA and APA guides for any formatting and style errors you may have made.

C

CONSTRUCTING PARAGRAPHS

A paragraph can be broadly defined as a group of sentences that are set off as a unit. The key qualities of a successful paragraph are unity, coherence, and emphasis. A *unified* paragraph focuses on one main idea, while a *coherent* paragraph consists of sentences that follow a clear and logical sequence. *Emphasis* refers to the means by which a writer engages and maintains the reader's interest.

C1 Sequencing Ideas

Some of the most common ways to sequence the ideas in a paragraph are these:

- from general to specific
  - topic to illustration
  - problem to solution
- from specific to general
  - illustration to topic
- from least important or complex to most important or complex
- from most important or familiar to least important or familiar
- according to time
- according to space

Part of your understanding of sequencing may come from the sorting activities (listing, mind-mapping, branching, outlining, and so forth) that you engage in during the prewriting stage. When constructing a paragraph, you need to decide what the paragraph's main claim (or thesis) is and how it relates to the rest of the paragraph. You typically present the main claim in your paragraph's *lead* or *topic sentence*. Although the main claim may appear in the middle of your paragraph, it usually comes at the beginning or end.

Ask yourself what the intent of your paragraph is. How does it relate to the paragraphs that precede and follow it? What transitions or links do you need to connect it to those paragraphs or to your topic? Your answers to these questions help you decide whether you want to start with your main claim and then support it with details or whether you want to start with one or more details and move to your main claim.

C2   Paragraph Purpose

One of the keys to writing is to keep your purpose in mind. A paragraph's pattern of organization will largely depend on the paragraph's purpose. Just as sentences can introduce, claim, argue, add detail, illustrate, define, review, link, or conclude, so too can paragraphs.

C3   Paragraph Development

There are a variety of different patterns of organization you can use to develop your paragraphs.

C3-a   Narration

A *narrative paragraph* tells you what happened or what is happening. To test the effectiveness of a narrative paragraph, ask the following questions:

- Is the illustration relevant or connected directly to the claim?
- Is the passage organized chronologically?
- Does the narrative show cause-and-effect relationships?
- Is the lead or topic sentence the key to understanding the narrative?

C3-b   Description

A *descriptive paragraph* sketches a portrait of a person, object, or event. To test the effectiveness of a descriptive paragraph, ask these questions:

- Are the description's various elements logically arranged?
- Do the primary elements of the description stand out?
- Does the description express a dominant point of view?

C3-c   Example

An *example* or *illustration paragraph* uses a specific example to illustrate a point. In an example paragraph, the example should be clearly stated and the point it is illustrating should be a valid one. An example paragraph must use concrete details to develop its illustration in a memorable or striking way.

C3-d Explanation

Paragraphs that explain can do so by process or by analogy. A *process paragraph* describes a sequence of actions, such as the steps involved in the tying of shoelaces. An *analogy paragraph* uses a familiar concept or process to help the reader understand an unfamiliar concept or process. Both approaches generate explanatory paragraphs.

C3-e Classification and Division

Classification groups items into categories on the basis of a common principle and explains that principle or applies it.

Division takes a single item and breaks it into parts, stating the rationale for this division.

C3-f Comparison and Contrast

When you *compare* two topics, you draw attention to their similarities. When you *contrast* two topics, you highlight their differences. A comparison and/or contrast paragraph may be structured in one of two ways. You may write of similarities/differences within a single paragraph or by addressing them in alternating paragraphs.

C3-g Definition

A *definition paragraph* establishes the meaning of a word or concept and may use means as varied as history and etymology to construct that definition.

C4 Paragraph Transitions

The connections between the sentences that make up a paragraph should be clear and logical. Transitions contribute to the coherence of a paragraph by indicating the precise relationships between sentences. Transitional devices include *transitional expressions, repetition,* and *parallel structure.*

C4-a Transitional Expressions

Transitional expressions are words or phrases that signal the connections between sentences. As the following list indicates, transitional expressions perform a variety of functions.

TO ADD
additionally, also, and, as well, besides, further, furthermore, in addition, moreover, too

TO GIVE AN EXAMPLE
for example, for instance, indeed, in fact, namely, specifically, such as, to illustrate

TO INDICATE CLARIFICATION
in other words, simply put, that is, to clarify, to put it simply

TO INDICATE SEQUENCE
afterward, and then, before, finally, first (second, third), following, immediately, in the first place, last, next

TO EMPHASIZE OR FOCUS
above all, even, indeed, in fact, in particular, more importantly, obviously, of course, specifically, that is, truly

TO COMPARE
again, also, by the same token, in the same manner, in the same way, just as . . . so too, likewise, similarly

TO CONTRAST
although, but, conversely, despite, even though, however, in contrast, in spite of, instead, nevertheless, nonetheless, notwithstanding, on the contrary, on the other hand, rather, still, though, whereas, yet

TO INDICATE CONCESSION
admittedly, although it is true that, granted that, naturally, of course, to be sure

TO INDICATE TIME
after, after a while, afterward, as, as long as, as soon as, at last, at that time, at this point, before, currently, during, earlier, eventually, finally, formerly, immediately, in the future, in the meantime, in the past, lately, later, meanwhile, next, now, presently, recently, shortly, simultaneously, since, so far, soon, subsequently, temporarily, then, thereafter, until, when, while

TO INDICATE PLACE OR DIRECTION
above, adjacent to, around, behind, below, beyond, close to, elsewhere, farther on, here, inside, near, nearby, opposite, there, to the left, to the right, under, underneath

TO INDICATE CAUSE AND EFFECT
accordingly, as a result, because, consequently, due to, for this purpose, for this reason, hence, since, so, then, therefore, thereupon, thus, to this end

19

TO REPEAT, SUMMARIZE, OR CONCLUDE
after all, all in all, all told, altogether, as a result, as mentioned, as noted, finally, hence, in brief, in conclusion, in other words, in short, in summary, in the final analysis, on the whole, that is, therefore, thus, to conclude, to summarize, to sum up

C4-b Repetition

Less common than the use of transitional expressions is the use of repetition to create transitions within paragraphs. The repeated element, which may be a word or phrase, functions as the paragraph's connective tissue.

C4-c Parallel Structure

Parallel structures—a series of words, phrases, or clauses that have the same grammatical function—bring coherence to a paragraph by emphasizing the connections between ideas.

For information about faulty parallel structure, see G3-d.

C5 Paragraph Structure

In the initial stages of constructing a paragraph, you are probably more concerned with clarifying your purpose and articulating your ideas than with deciding how your paragraph should be structured. You can increase the range of your composing choices, however, by becoming familiar with the structural patterns discussed in this section.

C5-a The Levels Concept

The concept of *levels* in paragraphs was introduced by the American composition theorist Francis Christensen.[1] This concept issues from the fact that, in successful paragraphs, a sentence is a single unit of thought. It cannot function on its own, however, and is necessarily connected to what comes before it and to what comes after. Christensen saw that a paragraph is created by combining sentences on different levels. The lead or topic sentence of a paragraph—the *level-one sentence* in Christensen's terms—contains the most general observation made in that paragraph about the paragraph's topic. A *level-two sentence* is a sentence that develops, in more detail, some

[1] See Francis Christensen, "A Generative Rhetoric of the Paragraph," in W. Ross Winterowd, ed., *Contemporary Rhetoric: A Conceptual Background with Readings* (New York: Harcourt Brace Jovanovich, 1975), 233–52.

part of what was said in the level-one sentence. A *level-three sentence* develops some aspect of what was conveyed in a level-two sentence.

Christensen argued that every sentence in a paragraph is either subordinate or coordinate. A sentence that relates to the sentence immediately preceding it performs a *subordinate* function by developing more precisely some aspect of that sentence. A sentence that relates to the lead sentence is *coordinate* with the other sentences in the paragraph that relate to that lead sentence. When the first sentence of a paragraph is the paragraph's lead sentence, the second sentence can be either subordinate or coordinate depending on its connection to the first sentence.

When you reason in your writing, Christensen observed, you do so principally by the methods of coordination and subordination. In coordination, a series of sentences develops a general observation; in subordination, each sentence represents a more detailed or exact development of an observation, image, or insight in the preceding sentence. Frequently, both coordination and subordination are used in a paragraph.

C5-b Coordinate, Subordinate, and Mixed Structures

Christensen's analysis showed that it is possible to use three kinds of paragraph structures: *coordinate, subordinate,* and *mixed*. In each paragraph that follows, the number preceding each sentence denotes the level of that sentence.

COORDINATE STRUCTURE

(1) The paragraph, as a composing unit, has been affected by three principal influences in the last century. (2) First, it has been shortened by the advent of mass printing and publication and the commercial wish to please everyone. (2) Second, it has simplified its diction considerably, partly because of a shift in taste and style, partly because of an increasing uncertainty about the abilities of the mass reader. (2) Finally, it has increasingly resorted to artificial modes of emphasis in an attempt to sustain the reader's attention.

SUBORDINATE STRUCTURE

(1) The paragraph, a basic unit of composition, was

severely influenced by the mass-production methods that came to dominate publishing in the last century. (2) Because the intended audience had increased tenfold and now included the barely literate as well as the rhetorically sophisticated, the paragraph grew shorter and shorter. (3) This condensing of average paragraph length was most notable in newspapers, where the narrow width of columns obscured the fact that most paragraphs had only a few sentences. (4) You should not be surprised, therefore, to learn that the average modern paragraph is less than half the length of a nineteenth-century paragraph.

MIXED STRUCTURE

(1) The paragraph, as a composing unit, has been affected by three principal influences in the last century. (2) It has been shortened by the advent of mass printing and publication and a wish to please everyone. (3) This shortening, gradual in the last part of the nineteenth century and the first quarter of the twentieth, was accelerated by Hemingway's example and the increasing influence of journalism. (2) The paragraph has also seen its diction simplified. (3) This can be attributed to shifts in both taste and style. (4) Certainly, the belief that plain speaking was honest speaking contributed to the dominance of a simpler vocabulary in the paragraph. (2) Finally, the paragraph came to cultivate increasingly artificial means of emphasis. (3) This is sharply evident in magazines appealing to teens where block letters, multiple exclamation marks, and direct, intimate address create a synthetically appealing style.

C6   Special-Purpose Paragraphs

In an essay, certain paragraphs perform unique tasks. The most important of these special-purpose paragraphs are introductory paragraphs, transitional paragraphs, and concluding paragraphs.

C6-a Introductory Paragraphs

The first paragraph of an essay is probably the most demanding of all to write. In the opening paragraph, you must introduce your topic and at the same time capture the attention or interest of your readers. You have the option in this paragraph of giving your readers a clear sense of the direction of your essay. These three functions are fulfilled by means of the hook, the thesis statement (or claim), and the preview.

HOOK

The term *hook* comes from the world of television. Scriptwriters in that medium must establish a strong opening to discourage channel-surfing. Techniques you can use to hook your readers include the following: a provocative quotation, an engaging anecdote, a powerful description, a strong statement, a memorable example, a thought-provoking question, an intriguing fact or statistic.

THESIS STATEMENT

A key element of the opening paragraph is the thesis statement or claim, a single sentence that conveys your essay's central point or idea. Opening paragraphs typically move from the general to the specific, concluding with the most specific sentence in the paragraph—the thesis. In such a construction, general statements lead to more specific statements and all of these prepare readers for the thesis statement.

PREVIEW

If you wish to give your readers a clear understanding of the direction your essay will take, you can include a preview in your opening paragraph. This element is optional. In an argument, for instance, you may elect not to present a preview because you may want your points, and the conclusion(s) you draw from them, to surprise the reader. A preview typically follows the thesis statement or claim.

C6-b Transitional Paragraphs

Transitional paragraphs are used to signal a major transition between ideas. A transitional paragraph typically performs three tasks: summarizing, emphasizing, and previewing. Use this kind of paragraph when you need a bridge between one topic and another. Use it sparingly, as it is the most elaborate of transition devices.

C6-c Concluding Paragraphs

The final paragraph of an essay fulfils three basic functions: (1) it summarizes the essay's key points; (2) it restates the claim or thesis; and (3) it indicates the general significance of the claim or thesis. In addition, a concluding paragraph should strike a note of finality; it should leave readers with the impression that nothing of importance has been left unsaid.

BASIC GRAMMAR

B1 Parts of Speech

Words can be divided into nine parts of speech: noun, pronoun, verb, adjective, adverb, conjunction, preposition, article, and interjection.

B1-a Nouns

Nouns are words that name persons, places, things, or ideas.

> The *focus group* was startled by the *revelation* that the *popcorn* sold in *theatres* contains more *fat* than a *hot dog.*

From this example and others you can study for yourself, certain properties of the noun should become clear.

1. Nouns are frequently preceded by words like *the, a, an, my, your, some, each, every, his, this,* and *that.*

2. The most traditional positions for nouns are before the verb, after the verb, and after a preposition.

3. Nouns may be singular or plural in number. The plural form of a noun is most frequently formed by adding *-s* or *-es* to the singular form. Some nouns have only one form for both the singular and the plural (*moose, moose*). Other nouns are irregular (*wife, wives*).

4. Nouns tend to have endings that distinguish them from verbs or adjectives: *-al, -ness, -ism, -ance, -ment.*

5. Nouns may function as subjects or objects. In the sentence *Shelley took the book from the shelf,* the noun *Shelley* is the subject, the noun *book* is the object, and the noun *shelf* is the object of the preposition *from.*

6. The apostrophe is used to form the possessive case of nouns (*Simpson's* lawn). The possessive case of singular nouns, including those that end in *-s,* is formed by adding *-'s* (*needle's* point, *Jones's* boat). The possessive case of plural nouns that end in *-s* is formed by adding only an apostrophe (*needles'* points).

7. Nouns can be classified into four categories according to the kind of entity they represent: a *common* noun names a general entity (*car*); a *proper* noun names a particular member of a class (*Chevrolet*); an *abstract* noun names a quality or idea that is not tangible (*beauty*); a *concrete* noun names something that is tangible (*grass*).

8. A collective noun names a group of entities, but its form is singular (*crowd*, *jury*, *team*, *committee*). A singular pronoun is used to replace a collective noun (a *team* and *its* record) unless that noun refers to individual members of the group (a *team* and *their* paycheques).

ESL *focus* COUNT AND NONCOUNT NOUNS

There are two classes of nouns in English: count and noncount. Count nouns name things that may be counted. They can be used with *one*, *a* or *an*, *the*, *many*, *several*, *some*, *few*, and *numbers*:

   five girls, several rocks, a few cities, many ideas

Singular count nouns cannot appear alone. They must follow an article or a demonstrative or possessive adjective:

   a book, the pen, his ear, their project, this feeling, that car

Plural count nouns can appear alone, with *the*, or with numbers:

   teachers, the teachers, ten teachers

Noncount nouns—which are sometimes called uncountable nouns or mass nouns—name things that are measured by their mass. They include some nouns that express abstraction:

   water, air, butter, gold, advice, anger, honesty, integrity

Noncount nouns cannot be used with *a* and *an*.

   a water, an air, an advice, an integrity

Noncount nouns can be used with *some*, *any*, or *more* to express quantity. They can also be connected to a count noun to specify an amount:

   any water, ten litres of water, some honesty

Most noncount nouns do not have a plural form:

   advice, equipment, information, money, traffic, water

Nouns such as *candy*, *cereal*, *cheese*, *chicken*, *chocolate*, *fish*, *paper*, and *wine* can be count or noncount depending on their function.

COUNT

   I ate *two candies*. [countable pieces of candy]

NONCOUNT

I like to eat *candy*. [general food type]

B1-b Pronouns

A pronoun is a word that takes the place of a noun. The noun that the pronoun replaces is known as the pronoun's *antecedent*.

Although the *country* is rich, *it* has high unemployment.

Pronouns fall into nine categories: personal, possessive, reflexive, intensive, demonstrative, relative, interrogative, indefinite, and reciprocal.

PERSONAL PRONOUNS

A personal pronoun refers to specific persons or things. Personal pronouns agree with their antecedents in number and gender, but their case depends on their function in a sentence. Table B-1 lists the 30 case forms of the personal pronoun. For more information about pronoun case, see U1.

TABLE B-1 Personal Pronouns

SINGULAR	SUBJECTIVE CASE	OBJECTIVE CASE	POSSESSIVE CASE
First person	I	me	my, mine
Second person	you	you	your, yours
Masculine	he	him	his
Feminine	she	her	her, hers
Neuter	it	it	its
PLURAL			
First person	we	us	our, ours
Second person	you	you	your, yours
Third person (all genders)	they	them	their, theirs

ESL *focus* PERSONAL PRONOUNS AND CASE

In English, *case* refers to the form a noun or pronoun takes to indicate its grammatical function in a sentence.

POSSESSIVE PRONOUNS

A possessive pronoun indicates ownership.

John lost *his* wallet.

REFLEXIVE PRONOUNS

Reflexive pronouns, which refer back to the subject of the sentence or clause in which they appear, are used to denote an action where the recipient and the doer are the same person or thing. A reflexive pronoun is formed by adding *-self* or *-selves* to a personal pronoun.

Did you hurt *yourself*?

INTENSIVE PRONOUNS

Intensive pronouns are used to emphasize a noun (or its equivalent). They have the same form as reflexive pronouns.

The voters spoke to the prime minister *himself*.

DEMONSTRATIVE PRONOUNS

A demonstrative pronoun identifies or points to a noun.

That is mine. This is ours.

RELATIVE PRONOUNS

A relative pronoun introduces an adjective clause (see B2-d) and refers to the noun or pronoun that the clause modifies.

The candidate *who* won the debate lost the election.

Tomas found the keys *that* he had misplaced.

The relative pronouns *who, whose,* and *whom* refer to people; *which* refers to inanimate objects, animals, and groups of persons; and *that* refers to either things or persons. For more information about *that* and *which*, see U2-b.

INTERROGATIVE PRONOUNS

An interrogative pronoun introduces a question. Interrogative pronouns include *who, whom, whose, which,* and *what*.

Which book won the Giller Prize?

Whose car is parked in the reserved space?

INDEFINITE PRONOUNS

An indefinite pronoun makes a reference to a nonspecific person or thing. Indefinite pronouns include *all, another, any, anyone, anything, each, everybody, everyone, everything, few, many, nobody, none, one, several, some,* and *somebody*.

Many of these words may function as either pronouns or adjectives. (See also G-2a.)

> Does *anyone* know the solution to the problem? [pronoun]

> *Each* client must pay a service fee. [adjective]

RECIPROCAL PRONOUNS

A reciprocal pronoun expresses a mutual relationship. There are only two reciprocal pronouns: *one another* and *each other*.

> The classmates smiled tentatively at *one another* on the first day.

B1-c Verbs

A verb is a word that expresses an action or a state of being. All verbs except *be* have four principal parts.

BASE FORM	I *open* the door.
PAST TENSE	I *opened* the door.
PAST PARTICIPLE	I have *opened* the door.
PRESENT PARTICIPLE	I am *opening* the door.

TRANSITIVE AND INTRANSITIVE VERBS

A *transitive* verb takes an object, while an *intransitive* verb does not. An object is needed to complete the meaning of a transitive verb.

TRANSITIVE	I *varnished* the table this afternoon. [The object *table* completes the meaning of the verb.]
INTRANSITIVE	The villagers *gathered* in the square. [The verb has no receiver.]

LINKING VERBS

A linking verb (V) connects the subject (S) with a *subject complement* (SC), a word or word group that identifies or describes the subject.

```
┌────────S────────┐ ┌─V─┐ ┌────────────SC────────────┐
Fuel cell technology seems a viable alternative to gasoline.
```

The most common linking verbs are *appear, become, feel, look, remain, seem, smell, sound, taste,* and forms of *be.*

TABLE B-2 Verb Tenses

PRESENT TENSE

SIMPLE PRESENT

The simple present indicates actions or conditions that are occurring now.

I stand	we stand
you stand	you stand
he, she, it stands	they stand

PRESENT PROGRESSIVE

The present progressive indicates actions or conditions that are ongoing.

I am standing	we are standing
you are standing	you are standing
he, she, it is standing	they are standing

PRESENT PERFECT

The present perfect indicates actions or conditions that began in the past and continue into the present.

I have stood	we have stood
you have stood	you have stood
he, she, it has stood	they have stood

PRESENT PERFECT PROGRESSIVE

The present perfect progressive indicates actions or conditions that began in the past, continue into the present, and may extend into the future.

I have been standing	we have been standing
you have been standing	you have been standing
he, she, it has been standing	they have been standing

PAST TENSE

SIMPLE PAST

The simple past indicates actions or conditions that occurred in the past.

I stood	we stood
you stood	you stood
he, she, it stood	they stood

PAST PROGRESSIVE

The past progressive indicates ongoing actions or conditions that occurred in the past.

I was standing	we were standing
you were standing	you were standing
he, she, it was standing	they were standing

PAST PERFECT

The past perfect indicates actions or conditions that occurred in the past and were completed before some other past actions or conditions occurred.

I had stood	we had stood
you had stood	you had stood
he, she, it had stood	they had stood

(continued)

31

TABLE B-2 Verb Tenses (cont.)

PAST PERFECT PROGRESSIVE	*The past perfect progressive indicates ongoing actions or conditions in the past that began before some other past actions or conditions began.*
I had been standing	we had been standing
you had been standing	you had been standing
he, she, it had been standing	they had been standing

FUTURE TENSE

SIMPLE FUTURE	*The simple future indicates actions or conditions that have yet to occur.*
I will stand	we will stand
you will stand	you will stand
he, she, it will stand	they will stand

FUTURE PROGRESSIVE	*The future progressive indicates ongoing actions or conditions that will occur in the future.*
I will be standing	we will be standing
you will be standing	you will be standing
he, she, it will be standing	they will be standing

FUTURE PERFECT	*The future perfect indicates actions or conditions that will be completed some definite time in the future.*
I will have stood	we will have stood
you will have stood	you will have stood
she, it will have stood	they will have stood

FUTURE PERFECT PROGRESSIVE	*The future perfect progressive indicates ongoing actions or conditions that will be completed by some definite time in the future.*
I will have been standing	we will have been standing
you will have been standing	you will have been standing
he, she, it will have been standing	they will have been standing

ESL *focus* HELPING VERBS

Helping verbs (also known as *auxiliary* verbs) combine with main verbs to indicate tense. The most common helping verbs are forms of *be, have,* and *do.*

The forms of *be* (*am, is, are, was,* and *were*) combine with the present-participle form of a verb (the *-ing* form) to create the progressive tense. The tense of the helping verb determines whether the past or present progressive tense is formed.

I *am* writing a letter to confirm our agreement.

The past-tense form of *be* combines with the past-participle form of a verb (the form ending in *-d*, *-ed*, *-n*, *-en*, or *-t*) to create the passive voice (see U5).

The letter *was* not *written* because of that interruption.

The forms of *do* are used to establish questions, emphasis, and negation.

QUESTION	*Do* you want to finish the letter?
EMPHASIS	I *did* want to finish that letter.
NEGATION	I *don't* know when I will finish it.

NOTE: For questions, use forms of *do* when forms of *be* are not part of the answer. (*Do* you know what he said? Yes, I *do*.) Use forms of *be* when forms of that verb are part of the answer. (*Are* you going to the party? Yes, I *am*.)

The forms of *have* combine with the past-participle form to create the perfect tense.

PRESENT PERFECT	I *have* finished the letter confirming our agreement.
PAST PERFECT	I *had* finished it before you arrived.
FUTURE PERFECT	I *will have* finished the letter before you arrive.

Modal auxiliaries are helping verbs that express obligation, necessity, probability, and ability. Unlike the forms of *be, have,* and *do,* modals do not change form to indicate tense. There are nine modals: *can, could, will, would, may, might, must, shall,* and *should.*

OBLIGATION	My brother *should* wash the car.
NECESSITY	My brother *must* wash the car.
PROBABILITY	My brother *may* wash the car.
ABILITY	My brother *can* wash the car.

IRREGULAR VERBS

Although most verbs in English follow a regular pattern, there are some two hundred irregular verbs. To learn how irregular verbs are conjugated, consult a dictionary.

VERBALS

A verbal is a verb form that does not function as a verb in a sentence. There are three kinds of verbals: infinitives, participles, and gerunds. *Infinitives* can function as nouns, adjectives, or adverbs.

NOUN	*To win* is gratifying.
ADJECTIVE	They had little opportunity *to respond.*
ADVERB	He waited *to see* the replay.

Participles, whether present or past, function as adjectives.

PRESENT PARTICIPLE	The *speeding* car was pulled over by the police.
PAST PARTICIPLE	The job required a *skilled* carpenter.

Gerunds have the same form as present participles, but they function in sentences as nouns.

GERUND	*Eating* is a necessity of life.

ESL*focus* GERUNDS AND INFINITIVES AFTER VERBS

A gerund is a verbal ending in *–ing* (*running, creating*). An infinitive is a verbal consisting of the base form of a verb preceded by *to* (*to run, to create*). Gerunds and infinitives that follow verbs function as direct objects (words or word groups that name the person or thing acted upon by the subject).

GERUND AS OBJECT	He enjoyed *winning* the race.
INFINITIVE AS OBJECT	She agreed *to run* for office.

Whether a gerund or an infinitive functions as the object in a sentence depends on the verb. Some verbs can be followed by a gerund but not by an infinitive. Other verbs can be followed by an infinitive but not by a gerund. Still other verbs can be followed by either a gerund or an infinitive.

VERBS FOLLOWED BY GERUND ONLY

admit	discuss	keep	recall
appreciate	enjoy	miss	regret
avoid	escape	postpone	risk
consider	finish	practise	stop
deny	imagine	quit	suggest

- I regretted *spending* the money.

VERBS FOLLOWED BY INFINITIVE ONLY

agree	expect	mean	promise
ask	have	need	refuse
beg	hope	offer	wait
claim	intend	plan	want
decide	manage	pretend	wish

- They need *to lower* their expectations.

VERBS FOLLOWED BY EITHER GERUND OR INFINITIVE

begin	hate	love	start
continue	like	prefer	try

- We began *counting* the votes. [gerund]
- We began to *count* the votes. [infinitive]

VOICE

The voice of a verb depends on whether the grammatical subject of the verb *acts* or is *acted upon*. If the subject acts, the verb is in the *active voice*; if it is acted upon, the verb is in the *passive voice*. (See also U5.)

ACTIVE VOICE   The quarterback *threw* the ball downfield. [The quarterback *acts*.]

PASSIVE VOICE   The quarterback *was sacked*. [The quarterback is *acted upon*.]

MOOD

Verbs may be cast in different moods depending on whether the writer wishes to make a factual statement *(indicative mood)*, give a command *(imperative mood)*, or express possibility rather than actuality *(subjunctive mood)*.

INDICATIVE   Toronto is in many respects the Chicago of Canada. [statement]

IMPERATIVE   Get me the evening newspaper. [command]

The subjunctive mood is more challenging. In the present subjunctive, the base form of the verb is used.

leave
They proposed that she ~~leaves~~ as soon as possible.
                       ^

35

be
It is essential that you ~~are~~ appointed to the committee.
    ^

In the past subjunctive, the form of *be* is *were*.

were
If I ~~was~~ you, I'd follow his advice.
  ^

FORMS OF THE SUBJUNCTIVE

Formal writing requires the use of the subjunctive mood in statements about hypothetical conditions; *that* clauses following verbs that request, order, or recommend; and dependent clauses (see B2-d) beginning with *as if* or *as though*.

Hypothetical conditions   The subjunctive mood is used to express a condition that is wished for or imagined.

were
If I was wealthy, I'd quit this stupid job.
  ^

That clauses   The subjunctive mood is used in *that* clauses following verbs such as *ask, command, insist, order, request, recommend,* and *suggest.*

accept
We recommend that the company accepts the deal.
        ^

As if, as though clauses   The subjunctive is used in *as if* and *as though* clauses, which express a hypothetical comparison.

were
The rookie politician delivered his speech as if he was a contestant in a speed-speaking event.
    ^

B1-d Adjectives and Adverbs

Adjectives and adverbs are words used to modify other words. Adjectives are easier to understand than adverbs, since they modify only nouns or pronouns.

The *gifted* pianist won the *international* competition.
[modify the nouns *pianist* and *competition*]

Adverbs modify verbs (or verbals), adjectives, other adverbs, or even entire clauses. Whereas adjectives answer the questions *which? what kind?* and *how many?*, adverbs specify *in what manner, where, when, why,* and *how much*.

We drove *slowly* around the block. [modifies the verb *drove*]

Antibiotics have proven to be an *extremely* important medical advance. [modifies the adjective *important*]

He plays the game *very* well. [modifies the adverb *well*]

Ironically, a spokesperson for the temperance association was charged with impaired driving. [modifies the entire clause]

COMPARATIVES AND SUPERLATIVES

When comparing two items, use the comparative form of the appropriate adjectives and adverbs.

Chocolate is *better* than licorice.

When comparing more than two items, use the superlative form of the appropriate adjectives and adverbs.

Of all candy, chocolate is *best*.

The comparative of one-syllable and some two-syllable adjectives is formed by adding *-er* and the superlative by adding *-est* (*large, larger, largest*). The comparative of many adjectives of two or more syllables is formed by adding *more* and the superlative by adding *most* (*careful, more careful, most careful; interesting, more interesting, most interesting*).

The comparative of adjectives ending in *-y* is formed by replacing the *-y* with *-ier* and the superlative by replacing the *-y* with *-iest*. Do not form double comparatives or double superlatives by adding *more* or *most* to these forms of the comparative and superlative (*happiest*, not *most happiest*).

He was the *happiest* [not the *most happiest*] person there.

The following adjectives and adverbs are irregular.

POSITIVE	COMPARATIVE	SUPERLATIVE
bad	worse	worst
badly	worse	worst
good	better	best
well	better	best
little	less	least
many	more	most
much	more	most
some	more	most

ESL*focus* INFINITIVES AND PARTICIPLES AS ADJECTIVES

In English, it is possible to use an infinitive or participle after certain verbs. When using *–ing* and *–ed* verbals as adjectives, be aware that your choice between the two endings will have a profound effect on the meaning of your statement.

The audience is *bored*. [The audience does not find the performance interesting.]

The audience is *boring*. [The audience does not stimulate the performer.]

CUMULATIVE AND COORDINATE ADJECTIVES

A series of adjectives can be cumulative or coordinate. A *cumulative* series is a sequence of adjectives in which each adjective modifies its successor (*light blue tweed material*). Note that the adjectives in a cumulative series are not separated by commas.

In a *coordinate* series, the adjectives all modify the same noun and are therefore separated by commas (*talented, industrious, ambitious entrepreneurs*). When coordinate adjectives are similar in nature, their order is unimportant (*smelly, overheated, humid room* and *overheated, smelly, humid room* are both acceptable). Order becomes an issue, however, when adjectives of different kinds occur in a series. You cannot say, for instance, *Norwegian, ten, fat, older gentlemen*. The following list will help you determine the correct order for your coordinate adjectives.

1. *Number or comparative or superlative form:* the, second, larger, smallest

2. *Evaluative adjective:* sour, dedicated, handsome

3. *Size:* huge, tiny, long

4. *Shape:* rectangular, round, ovoid

5. *Age:* old, young, eighteenth–century

6. *Colour:* magenta, green, scarlet

7. *Nationality:* Swedish, Canadian, Filipino

8. *Religion:* Muslim, Protestant, Jewish

9. *Material:* ceramic, pewter, wood

10. *Noun as adjective:* faculty lounge, student centre

ESL *focus* PLACEMENT OF ADVERBS

The placement of adverbs can cause ESL writers difficulty. By mastering a few rules, however, you can overcome that difficulty.

1. The position of an adverb is determined by what kind of adverb it is.

   a. Adverbs of *manner* (how a task is done) appear at the beginning or end of the sentence.

      I *quickly* bent my mind to the task.

      I bent my mind to the task *quickly*.

   b. Adverbs of *time* are placed at the beginning or end of the sentence.

      In the morning, I eat lightly.

      I eat lightly *in the morning.*

   c. Adverbs of *place* appear at the end of the sentence.

      He opened the door and went *into the room.*

   d. Adverbs of *degree or emphasis* are placed directly in front of the word they modify.

      He is *almost* ready to go to the game.

   e. Adverbs of *frequency* are placed in the middle if they modify the verb and at the beginning if they modify the sentence.

      She *always* likes to play golf.

      Usually, she is early for her tee time.

2. An adverb that modifies an adjective or another adverb is placed before the word it modifies.

   Tuition is *extremely* high. [modifies the adjective *high*]

   EXCEPTION: The adverb *enough* always follows the adjective or adverb it modifies.

   She dances well *enough*.

   Do not place an adverb between a transitive verb and its direct object.

   INCORRECT   He threw *quickly* the ball to the catcher.

   REVISED   He *quickly* threw the ball to the catcher.

B1-e Conjunctions

Conjunctions link words or word groups to one another and show the relationship between the elements connected.

COORDINATING CONJUNCTIONS

Coordinating conjunctions (*and, but, yet, or, for, not, so*) join grammatically equal words, phrases, or clauses.

Shirley *and* Joseph have never got past their initial dislike of each other. [joins the words *Shirley* and *Joseph*]

You can park the scooter on the street *or* in the garage. [joins the phrases *on the street* and *in the garage*]

He didn't like the play, *so* he left. [joins the clauses *He didn't like the play* and *he left*]

SUBORDINATING CONJUNCTIONS

Subordinating conjunctions introduce dependent, or subordinate, clauses (B2-d) and show the relationship between those clauses and independent clauses (B2-c).

I couldn't risk leaving him alone *because* his despair seemed bottomless.

Following is a list of common subordinating conjunctions:

after	even though	so that	when
although	if	than	whenever
as	in order that	that	where
as if	once	though	whereas
because	rather than	unless	wherever
before	since	until	while

CORRELATIVE CONJUNCTIONS

Correlative conjunctions are pairs of conjunctions that join equal words or word groups.

both/and	neither/not	not only/but also
either/or	not/but	whether/or

The joined words or word groups should be parallel grammatical elements.

We have *neither* the time *nor* the inclination to respond.

For information about faulty parallel structure, see G3-d.

B1-f Prepositions

Prepositions are connecting words that show the relationships between nouns or pronouns and other words in a sentence. A preposition can signal space and time (*above, below, near, after, before, until*), cause (*since, due to*), or exclusion (*except, but*).

SPACE   The smokestack is *near* the river.

TIME   They went home *after* the show.

CAUSE   Due to the fact that it's likely to rain, we should find shelter.

EXCLUSION   Everyone *but* Mr. Kwan signed.

There are fewer than one hundred prepositions in English. Some common prepositions are listed below.

about	before	during	off
above	behind	except	on
across	below	for	onto
after	beside	from	out
against	between	in	over
among	beyond	inside	past
around	by	into	toward
as	concerning	near	under
at	down	of	within

B1-g Articles

There are three articles in English—*a, an,* and *the.* An article works like an adjective in that it appears before a noun and indicates either a specific version or a generic version of that noun.

SPECIFIC   The children set *the* table.

GENERIC   We want to purchase *a* table.

The correct use of *a* and *an* depends on the initial sound, not letter, of the word that follows. *A* should be used before all words beginning with a consonant sound and a sounded *h*. *An* appears before words beginning with a vowel sound or a silent *h*.

a computer	an apple
a European	an hour
a historian	an uncle

ESL *focus* ARTICLES AND NOUNS

Articles can be a problem if your first language does not use articles before nouns. English, like other romance languages, uses articles in specific ways, but not all romance languages use articles in the way that English does.

The article *the* precedes nouns that are specific; the articles *a* and *an* are used to mark nouns that are nonspecific.

SPECIFIC   He is *the first* person to win the game.

NONSPECIFIC   He saw *a person* enter the house.

WHEN TO USE *THE*

with names of countries that include such words as *kingdom, state, republic*, and *union*
- the Republic of South Africa

with plural proper nouns
- the Rocky Mountains, the Toronto Maple Leafs, the United Nations, the Fongs

with names of oceans, seas, rivers, gulfs, canals, and deserts
- the Atlantic, the Red River, the Sahara Desert

with names of languages and proper names that include *of* in their title
- the English language, the University of Manitoba

WHEN NOT TO USE AN ARTICLE

with nonspecific plural nouns and noncount nouns
- *Dogs* are good household pets.

with singular proper names
- John Smith, Dr. Mai Leung, Prime Minister Macdonald, Quebec

Exception
- My Canada is a Canada that is tolerant of cultural diversity.

with fields of study, names of diseases, and names of newspapers, magazines, and periodicals that do not have an article in the title
- geography, measles, *Maclean's* magazine

B1-h Interjections

Interjections are isolated words or phrases that express emotion. They can stand alone as complete sentences or they can be connected to another sentence. If connected to another sentence, they are usually set off by punctuation marks. Exclamation marks set off intense interjections, while commas are used for mild interjections.

Hey! What do you think you're doing?

Oh well, at least you tried.

B2 Phrases and Clauses

A phrase is a group of words that functions as a noun, verb, or modifier; phrases cannot stand alone because they do not include both a subject (S1-a) and a predicate (S1-b). A clause is a group of words that contains both a subject and a predicate. There are two types of clauses: *dependent clauses*, which do not make a complete statement, and *independent clauses*, which do.

B2-a Prepositional Phrases

A prepositional phrase consists of a preposition, its object, and any modifiers of the object. Although prepositional phrases usually function as adjectives or adverbs, they can function as subjects as well.

ADJECTIVE   I hear the sparrows *in the trees.*

ADVERB   *From their perches* they sing.

SUBJECT   *In the trees* seems a happy place to be.

B2-b Verbal Phrases

Verb forms that function as modifiers and nouns rather than verbs are called verbals; they include present participles (the *-ing* form of a verb), past participles (the form of the verb ending in *-ed*, *-d*, *-en*, *-n*, or *-t*), and infinitives (the base form of a verb preceded by *to*). A verbal phrase consists of a verbal with any modifiers, objects, or complements. There are three kinds of verbal phrases: participle, gerund, and infinitive.

PARTICIPLE PHRASES

Participle phrases consist of either present participles or past participles, and always function as adjectives.

Canadians *travelling abroad* need a valid passport.

Drenched to the skin, Mai admitted she should have carried an umbrella.

GERUND PHRASES

Present participles (verbals ending in *-ing*) that function as nouns are called gerunds. A gerund phrase is made up of a gerund with any modifier, object, or complement.

John likes *being a good student.* [object of the verb]

INFINITIVE PHRASES

Infinitive phrases consist of an infinitive (*to see, to think, to kick, to be*) with any modifiers, objects, or complements. They can function as nouns, adjectives, or adverbs.

When he received the award, the controversial director began *to feel vindicated.* [object of the verb]

Travelling *to observe other cultures* can be an edifying experience. [adjective modifying *Travelling*]

I laughed *to relieve my tension.* [adverb modifying *laughed*]

OTHER PHRASES: APPOSITIVE PHRASES

Appositives and appositive phrases identify or describe the nouns or pronouns that immediately precede them. The two types of appositives—restrictive and nonrestrictive—differ in their use of commas. A *restrictive appositive* is not set off with commas because it defines or limits the meaning of the noun or pronoun it names; it contains essential information and therefore could not be removed from the sentence. A *nonrestrictive appositive* is set off with commas because the information it contains is nonessential—that is, it expands on the meaning of the noun or pronoun but could be removed from the sentence without changing the basic meaning.

RESTRICTIVE   My sister *Tracy* is often afflicted with migraine. [The speaker has more than one sister.]

NONRESTRICTIVE   My sister, *Tracy,* is often afflicted with migraine. [Tracy is the speaker's only sister.]

ABSOLUTE PHRASES

Absolute phrases are made up of nouns and participles, together with any modifiers or objects. An absolute phrase modifies an entire sentence or clause and is set off from the rest of the sentence with commas.

Her voice shaking with anger, she dismissed him.

B2-c Independent Clauses

An independent clause is a group of words that contains both a *subject* and a *predicate* and can stand alone as a complete sentence.

The plane landed.

B2-d Dependent Clauses

Dependent clauses (also known as *subordinate clauses*) contain both a *subject* and a *predicate* but cannot stand alone as complete sentences. A dependent clause functions within a sentence as an adverb, an adjective, or a noun.

ADVERB CLAUSES

Adverb clauses modify adjectives, adverbs, or words or groups of words that function as verbs. They begin with a subordinating conjunction and answer the questions *how, where, when,* or *why.*

When she reads the stock market report, Mel often finds new investment possibilities. [modifies a verb]

ADJECTIVE CLAUSES

Adjective clauses (also known as *relative clauses*) modify nouns or pronouns. They begin with a relative pronoun (*who, whom, whose, whoever, whomever, that, which, whichever, what,* or *whatever*) or a relative adverb (*when, where, whether,* or *why*).

The boy *who won the free tickets to the concert* was standing right in front of the stage when his name was called. [relative pronoun as subject of clause]

The car that was prominently featured in one of the early James Bond films was an Aston Martin. [restrictive clause]

Henry Ford's Model T, *which remained in production for twenty years,* transformed Ford Motors. [nonrestrictive clause]

NOUN CLAUSES

Noun clauses function as subjects, direct objects, objects of prepositions, or subject complements. They begin with a relative pronoun (*who, whom, whose, whoever, whomever, that, which, whichever, what, whatever*) or with *when, where, whether, why,* or *how.* A noun clause can also function as an appositive and rename (identify or explain) a noun.

Whoever refuses to study courts disaster. [subject]

A business needs to know *what its customers want.*
[direct object]

The fact *that Mario had already seen the film* did not
deter him from seeing it again. [appositive]

SENTENCE ELEMENTS

S1   Parts of Sentences

The two main parts of a sentence are the subject and the predicate.

S1-a   Subjects

The *simple subject* (SS) of a sentence is a noun or pronoun that carries out an action, is acted upon, or has something said about it.

> SS
> The *airplane* made an emergency landing.

A *complete subject* is made up of the simple subject and all the words that modify it.

> ┌─────── COMPLETE SUBJECT ───────┐
> ╲ SS
> *The airplane with the damaged engine* made an
> emergency landing.

A *compound subject* consists of two or more simple subjects joined by a coordinating conjunction or a correlative conjunction. (For information about coordinating and correlative conjunctions, see B1-e.)

> ┌── COMPOUND ──┐
> │   SUBJECT   │
> ┌─ SS ────── SS ─┐
> *Trudeau* and *Lévesque* were political adversaries.

There are a variety of constructions in which the subject does not appear at the beginning of the sentence. In commands, the subject *you* is understood but not stated.

> SS
> [You] Get the ball!

In questions, the position of the subject changes.

> SS
> Why do *you* want to see that movie?

Sentences that begin with *there* can create confusion. *There* is not the subject of the sentence; it merely points to the subject that follows the verb.

> SS
> There is *Costa* over by the piano.

S1-b   Predicates

The *simple predicate* (SP) of a sentence is the main verb.

        SP
Elvis Stojko *skated*.

A *complete predicate* consists of the main verb and its modifiers, together with any objects or complements and their modifiers.

```
                  ── COMPLETE PREDICATE ──
   ┌ SP
```
Elvis Stojko *skated to music from a film about Bruce Lee.*

A *compound predicate* consists of two or more verbs that have the same subject and are joined by a coordinating conjunction or a correlative conjunction.

```
                ── COMPOUND PREDICATE ──
   ┌ SP              SP
```
The forward *stole the puck, dashed down the ice, and scored.*

S1-c   Direct and Indirect Objects

A *direct object* (DO) is a word or word group that names the person or thing acted upon by the subject (S). It answers the questions *what?* or *whom?* about the verb (V).

     S   V   DO
The dog bit *the man*.

An *indirect object* (IO) is a noun or pronoun that answers the question *for whom?*, *to whom?*, *to what?*, or *for what?* about the verb.

S   V   IO   ┌─ DO ─┐
Sam gave *you the tickets*.

When both objects are present in a sentence, the indirect object usually precedes the direct object.

         IO   ┌── DO ──┐
Marie-Claire lent *me the dictionary*.

EXCEPTIONS: The direct object precedes the indirect object (1) when the indirect object is placed in a prepositional phrase;

     ┌── DO ──┐   ┌─IO ─┐
She sent *the package* to *her cousin*.

and (2) in sentences with the verbs *explain, describe, say, mention,* or *open.*

	IO ⌐— DO —⌐
INCORRECT	Loa explained *Signe the concept.*

	⌐— DO —⌐ IO
REVISED	Loa explained *the concept* to *Signe.*

S1-d Subject and Object Complements

A *subject complement* (SC) is a word or word group that follows a *linking verb* (forms of *be* and verbs such as *seem, appear, become, grow, remain, stay, prove, feel, look, smell, sound,* and *taste*) and identifies or describes the subject.

⌐——— S ———⌐   V   ⌐——— SC ———⌐
The company remains *a solid investment.*

An *object complement* is a word or group that follows a direct object and identifies or describes that object.

S   V ⌐— DO —⌐ OC
Natasha called Raj's project *superb.*

S2 Sentence Patterns

S2-a Pattern 1: Subject–verb

The simplest sentence pattern you can use is the subject–verb pattern. All that is necessary to complete this pattern is a subject and an *intransitive verb* (the kind of verb that takes no object).

S   V   S   V
Birds fly.   Fish swim.

S2-b Pattern 2: Subject–verb–subject complement

Pattern 2 uses a linking verb (forms of *be* and verbs such as *appear, become, feel, grow, look, make, seem, smell,* and *sound*) to connect a subject to its complement. A *subject complement* is a word or word group that identifies or describes the subject.

```
  ┌─S─┐  V      SC          S   V ┌─SC─┐
```
That pie smells delicious.   She is a lawyer.

S2-c   Pattern 3: Subject–verb–direct object

The verb in pattern 3 is the *transitive verb*, which transmits its action from a subject to an object.

```
┌───── S ─────┐ ┌─V─┐┌── DO ──┐
```
William and Mary drank a bottle of wine.

To better understand transitive verbs, think of the subject and transitive verb as asking the questions *who* or *what?* and the direct object as answering either question.

What did William and Mary drink? *A bottle of wine.*

S2-d   Pattern 4: Subject–verb–indirect
object–direct object

Pattern 4 includes two objects: the direct object, which names the receiver of the action; and the indirect object, which identifies *to whom* or *to what* the action is done.

```
     S        V     ┌── IO ──┐┌── DO ──┐
```
The instructor assigns his students weekly tests.

S2-e   Pattern 5: Subject–verb–direct
object–object complement

Pattern 5 includes an object complement, which identifies or describes the direct object named by the transitive verb.

```
┌───S ───┐  V     DO  ┌──OC ──┐
```
The curling club named Gordon bonspiel chair.

S3   Sentence Grammar

Grammatically, sentences are classified as *simple, compound, complex,* and *compound-complex.*

S3-a   Simple Sentences

A simple sentence consists of one independent clause with no dependent clauses. The subject and/or predicate of the independent clause may be compound.

Dick walked.

Until recently, Dick and Jane walked to the corner store and bought some candy every Saturday morning.

S3-b Compound Sentences

A compound sentence consists of two or more independent clauses with no dependent clauses. The clauses may be joined by a semicolon or a comma and a coordinating conjunction (*and, but, or, nor, for, or, yet*).

INDEPENDENT
┌─INDEPENDENT CLAUSE ─┐ ┌   CLAUSE   ┐
The evidence is overwhelming; it cannot be denied.

┌─INDEPENDENT CLAUSE ─┐ ┌─INDEPENDENT CLAUSE─┐
They want to go to Australia, but they can't afford the airfare.

S3-c Complex Sentences

A complex sentence is composed of one independent clause (IC) with at least one dependent clause (DC).

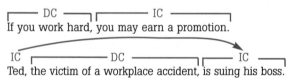

┌──── DC ────┐ ┌────── IC ──────┐
If you work hard, you may earn a promotion.

IC ┌────── DC ──────┐ ┌── IC ──┐
Ted, the victim of a workplace accident, is suing his boss.

The complex sentence is formed through subordination, with one clause placed in a subordinate relationship to another clause.

S3-d Compound-Complex Sentences

A compound–complex sentence consists of two or more independent clauses and at least one dependent clause.

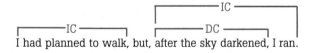

┌────── IC ──────┐
┌──IC──┐ ┌── DC ──┐
I had planned to walk, but, after the sky darkened, I ran.

S4 Sentence Purposes

S4-a Classification

Sentences can be classified in terms of the purposes they fulfil. *Declarative* sentences make a statement, *interrogative* sentences ask a question, *imperative* sentences convey a command, and *exclamatory* sentences express strong emotion.

DECLARATIVE	Mike Weir won the tournament.
INTERROGATIVE	Did you see *The Lord of the Rings?*
IMPERATIVE	Finish the report today.
EXCLAMATORY	What a sore loser she is!

S4-b Formation of Interrogative Sentences

Interrogative sentences can be direct or indirect. A *direct question* asks a question directly and ends with a question mark. An *indirect question* is phrased differently: it reports rather than asks a question and is followed by a period.

| DIRECT | Are the winters long in Manitoba? |
| INDIRECT | She asked whether the winters were long in Winnipeg. |

Declarative sentences with forms of the verb *to be* (*am, is, are, was,* and *were*) can be converted into direct questions by reversing the order of the subject and the verb.

| DECLARATIVE | Increasing numbers of homeless people are sleeping on the street. |
| DIRECT | Are increasing numbers of homeless people sleeping on the street? |

In direct questions that begin with *who, whom,* or *what,* the word order is determined by the case that is being used. If the subjective case is used, the subject (*who* or *what*) precedes the verb. If the objective case is used, the object (*whom* or *what*) appears before both the subject and the verb.

| SUBJECTIVE | Who took the candy? |
| OBJECTIVE | Whom did the voters elect? |

S5 Sentence Variety

You can achieve variety in your writing by combining sentences, creating different sentence types, and making use of emphasis and contrast.

S5-a   Combining Sentence Elements

When you write, you are constantly creating relationships, assessing ideas, and determining priorities. In making these decisions, you are carrying out some of the basic planning and organizing of your work, but you are also determining whether an idea is coordinate (of equal value) or subordinate (of lesser value). This determination helps you to decide whether to combine particular sentence elements or leave them independent of each other.

Combining sentence elements can be as simple as joining subjects and predicates.

COMBINING SUBJECTS

Toronto has become a metropolis.

Montreal has become a metropolis.

Toronto and Montreal have become metropolises.

COMBINING PREDICATES

The football team runs the ball well.

The football team passes the ball well.

The football team runs and passes the ball well.

You can combine two independent clauses of equal importance by linking them with a comma and a coordinating conjunction (*and, but, so, for, or, nor, yet*).

┌──────── INDEPENDENT CLAUSE ────────┐
Kim Campbell was Canada's first female prime minister,

┌──── INDEPENDENT CLAUSE ────┐
but she was in office for only a short time.

If you were to decide that one independent clause is subordinate, you would rewrite it as a dependent clause.

┌──────────── DEPENDENT CLAUSE ────────┐
Although Kim Campbell was Canada's first female prime

────┐┌──── INDEPENDENT CLAUSE ────┐
minister, she was in office for only a short time.

Instead of combining the two sentences about Campbell through either coordination or subordination, you could express the fact that Campbell was Canada's first female prime minister as an appositive phrase (see B2-b). The appositive phrase in the following example sentence makes the brevity of Campbell's tenure the most important point.

┌────── APPOSITIVE PHRASE ──────┐
Kim Campbell, Canada's first female prime minister, was in office for only a short time.

S5-b Forming Different Sentence Types

The following passage consists of simple sentences. As you read the passage, notice how choppy the flow of ideas is.

TOO CHOPPY   Canada has many colourful place names. Some seem strange to us today. We do not remember the origin of those names. Baies de Ha Ha, Quebec, is a good example. Ha Ha comes from the old French word for dead end: *haha*.

To eliminate the choppiness in this passage, you could combine the second and third sentences to create a compound sentence and join the last three sentences to form a complex sentence.

REVISED   Canada has many colourful place names. Some of them seem strange to us today, for we do not remember the origin of those names [*compound sentence*]. Baies de Ha Ha, Quebec, is a good example. Ha Ha comes from the old French word for dead end: *haha*.

You could transform the passage further by combining the first two sentences in the revised version to form a compound-complex sentence.

REVISED   Although Canada has many colourful place names, some of them seem strange to us today, for we do not remember the origin of those names.

S5-c Establishing Emphasis and Contrast

One way to keep your readers engaged is to introduce emphasis and contrast into your sentences. You can do so by *varying the lengths of your sentences, using periodic sentences where appropriate,* and *creating parallel structures.*

VARYING SENTENCE LENGTHS

The following passage consists of seven short sentences and a concluding long sentence. The long sentence derives much of its power from the contrast between its length and that of the sentences that precede it.

Jacques Parizeau puzzled veteran political observers. He was unusually rumpled and ungainly in appearance. He lacked the lean modern look of a Romanow. His press conferences were masterpieces of indirection. His eyes twinkled. His words alternately illuminated and obscured. This mystery, however, was not a genuine riddle. *For Parizeau, unlike his contemporaries, was motivated not by a wish to gain and retain power but by a dream of a unified and sovereign Quebec making its entry on the world stage.*

LOOSE AND PERIODIC SENTENCES

A loose or cumulative sentence begins with the subject and the predicate and then accumulates information as it progresses.

LOOSE   *The ferry gently nosed into the dock,* the line of its journey still visible in its broadening wake.

In contrast, a periodic sentence builds to its main idea by not revealing the subject and predicate until the end.

PERIODIC   The line of its journey still visible in its broad-ening wake, *the ferry gently nosed into the dock.*

You should use the periodic sentence sparingly. It is particu-larly effective in situations where you wish to place emphasis on the main idea in the independent clause.

PARALLELISM

Parallelism in a sentence is created by repeating grammatical elements, whether words, phrases, or entire clauses. Parallel structures give your writing a special kind of emphasis because they contain both repeating elements and changing elements. See how the phrase *They worried that* in the pas-sage about the Toronto Blue Jays establishes a repeating (or parallel) element and grants extra emphasis to the parts of each sentence that are different.

The Blue Jays, after years of defeats at crucial moments, were worried heading into another series at the end of a long season. *They worried that,* again, the winning plays would be made by the other team, the timely hits would rattle exclusively off opposition bats. *They worried that* a jinx had been created, born of letdowns at crucial moments in their previous playoffs. They worried needlessly.

For more information about parallelism, see C4-c and G3-d.

G

GRAMMATICAL SENTENCES

G1 Construction

A sentence is an independent clause, a group of words that contains both a subject and a predicate. The subject names the thing or person that the sentence is about. The predicate consists of the verb and any object, modifier, or complement of the verb. (For more information about subjects and predicates, see S1-a and S1-b.)

```
┌─── SUBJECT ───┐  ┌─────── PREDICATE ───────┐
```
Steven King's fiction has influenced horror films.

G1-a Sentence Fragments

A sentence fragment is a word group that, for various reasons, fails to qualify as a sentence. For example, there may be no subject or no predicate.

NO SUBJECT | Having crossed the Pacific. [Who crossed the Pacific?]

NO PREDICATE | The first Chinese, who came from California in 1858. [What did the Chinese do?]

In a third kind of fragment, both a subject and a predicate are present, but they are preceded by a subordinating conjunction.

Since the Barenaked Ladies started to become popular in the United States. [What *happened* since they started to become popular?]

CORRECTING SENTENCE FRAGMENTS

A fragment that lacks a *subject* can be corrected by adding a subject or by combining the fragment with an independent clause.

FRAGMENT | Having crossed the Pacific.

REVISED | Having crossed the Pacific, the first known Japanese immigrant to Canada settled in Victoria in 1877. [combined with independent clause]

A fragment that lacks a *predicate* can be corrected by adding a predicate or by combining the fragment with an independent clause.

FRAGMENT   The first Chinese, who came from
                California in 1858.

REVISED   The first Chinese, who came from
                California in 1858, were looking for gold.
                [predicate added]

ESL *focus* MISSING SUBJECTS AND VERBS

You may be familiar with a language that allows the
omission of an explicit subject or verb if the sentence is
clear without it. Such an omission is not permitted in
English, however. For that reason, the following examples
are fragments, not sentences.

MISSING SUBJECT   Has asked for plans for two new
                   parks.

MISSING VERB   Winnipeggers very outgoing.

To revise these fragments, add the subjects and verbs required
to complete the sentence.

City council has
Has ˄asked for plans for two new downtown parks.

               are
Winnipeggers ˄very outgoing.

EXCEPTION: The imperative sentence, which expresses a
command, need not include a stated subject. For example,
in the sentence *Clean up your room*, the subject *you* is
assumed, not stated.

If the fragment is a phrase or a dependent clause, either combine it with an independent clause or turn it into an independent clause.

FRAGMENT   In 1870 by the Icelandic community.

REVISED   In Manitoba, women's suffrage was first
                proposed in 1870 by the Icelandic
                community. [phrase combined with an
                independent clause]

Most fragmented dependent clauses are partial thoughts
that have been unintentionally separated from a nearby sentence where they belong. To correct such fragments, simply
join the two parts.

FRAGMENT   Canadian women felt cheated. When the federal government extended voting rights in 1917 only to women in the armed services and to female relatives of men in the military.

REVISED   Canadian women felt cheated when, in 1917, the federal government extended voting rights only to women in the armed services and to female relatives of men in the military.

ESL *focus* VERBAL-PHRASE FRAGMENTS

A special type of fragment results when the writer assumes that a verbal phrase can take the place of a verb.

FRAGMENT   The candidate, *having learned* that he was trailing in the polls, and *knowing* that he would have a hard time catching up in the last week.

You may think the above example is a complete sentence because it contains words that sound like verbs. However, *having learned* and *knowing* are verbals, not verbs. The clause has a subject (*the candidate*) but no predicate because it has no verb. Adding a predicate would complete the sentence.

REVISED   *The candidate,* having learned that he was trailing in the polls, and knowing that he would have a hard time catching up in the last week, *launched a series of hard-hitting television advertisements.*

G1-b Run-On Sentences

Run-on sentences consist of independent clauses that have not been joined correctly. They fall into two categories: the *fused sentence* and the *comma splice.*

FUSED SENTENCES

When two independent clauses are joined with no punctuation or connecting word between them, the result is a fused sentence.

FUSED SENTENCE   Constance loves to read she often
                        falls asleep at night with a book
                        pressed to her nose.

To correct a fused sentence, you have the following options:

1. Make the two independent clauses into separate sentences.

    Constance loves to read. She often falls asleep at
    night with a book pressed to her nose.

2. Link the clauses with a comma and a coordinating
    conjunction (*and, but, yet, or, for, nor, so*).

    Constance loves to read, *so* she often falls asleep at
    night with a book pressed to her nose.

3. Link the clauses with a semicolon or with a semicolon
    followed by a conjunctive adverb.

    Constance loves to read; *consequently,* she often
    falls asleep at night with a book pressed to her
    nose.

4. Turn one of the independent clauses into a dependent
    clause.

    Because Constance loves to read, she often falls
    asleep at night with a book pressed to her nose.

5. Turn the two clauses into a single independent clause.

    Constance's passion for reading sometimes causes
    her to fall asleep at night with a book pressed to
    her nose.

COMMA SPLICES

A comma splice occurs when two independent clauses are
joined with only a comma. You can correct a comma splice by
using any of the options used to correct a fused sentence.

COMMA SPLICE   Michael Ondaatje's novel *The English
                 Patient* was a critical and popular success,
                 it was made into a movie.

G2 Agreement

G2-a Subject–Verb Agreement

A verb must agree with its subject in number (singular or plural) and in person (first, second, or third). Consider, for example, the present-tense forms of the verb *see*.

	SINGULAR	PLURAL
FIRST PERSON	I see	we see
SECOND PERSON	you see	you see
THIRD PERSON	he/she/it sees	they see

SUBJECTS WITH *AND*

Most compound subjects joined by *and* are plural and therefore require a plural verb.

Geneviève and Cloë ~~is~~ *are* going to the dance next Saturday.

Two linked subjects that are viewed as a single unit take a singular verb.

Strawberries and Cream ~~are~~ *is* Marsha's favourite ice-cream.

WORDS OR PHRASES BETWEEN SUBJECT AND VERB

Words or phrases that come between the subject and the verb can cause confusion.

One of the students ~~were~~ *was* writing a report on the effectiveness of Canada's policy on multiculturalism.

In the preceding example, the subject is *one*, not *students*. *Students* is part of the phrase *of the students*, which modifies the noun (and subject) *one*.

When a singular subject is followed by a phrase beginning with *as well as, in addition to, together with,* or a similar construction, the verb should agree with the singular subject, not with the subject in the intervening phrase.

John, together with his classmates, ~~think~~ *thinks* that Arnold Schwarzenegger has not made a good movie since *Terminator 2*.

SUBJECTS JOINED BY *OR* OR *NOR*

When a compound subject is joined by *or* or *nor*, make the verb agree with the part of the subject closest to the verb.

Customs or *tradition shapes* everyday behaviour.

Tradition or *customs shape* everyday behaviour.

When a singular subject and a plural subject are joined by *either/or* or *neither/nor,* you can avoid awkwardness by placing the plural subject closest to the verb.

AWKWARD   Either the *passengers* or the *driver is* responsible for the accident.

REVISED   Either the *driver* or the *passengers are* responsible for the accident.

INDEFINITE PRONOUNS AS SUBJECTS

Indefinite pronouns such as *one, none, each, either, neither, another, anyone,* and *anything* refer to nonspecific persons or things and are singular in meaning. The indefinite pronouns *everyone, everybody,* and *everything* are also singular even though they appear to be plural in meaning. (See also B-1b.)

        is
Everybody are excited that the Expos are in first place.

Some indefinite pronouns, including *all, any,* and *some,* can be either singular or plural, depending on the noun they refer to.

SINGULAR   *Some* of the instructor's *lesson* is hard to understand.

PLURAL   *Some instructors* are hard to understand.

COLLECTIVE NOUNS AS SUBJECTS

Collective nouns such as *class, family, team, committee, audience, couple,* and *group* can take either a singular or a plural verb, depending on whether they function as a single unit or as individual members of a unit.

SINGULAR   The *jury has* returned a verdict of guilty.
                     [functions as single unit]

PLURAL   The *jury are* debating the evidence.
                     [function as individual members of unit]

The names of companies are collective nouns. Most company names with plural or compound forms take singular verbs.

Brooks Brothers *is* seeking to expand its customer base.

For more information about collective nouns, see G2-c.

SUBJECT COMPLEMENTS

A verb should agree with the subject, not with the subject complement.

> *were*
> Excessive absences was the reason for the employee's dismissal.

In the preceding example sentence, the plural subject *absences* is linked to the singular complement *reason* by the plural verb *were*. If the subject and complement in this sentence were reversed, the verb would be singular.

> *was*
> The reason for the employee's dismissal were excessive absences.

For more information about subject complements, see S1-d.

INTRODUCTORY *THERE*

In sentences beginning with *There*, the number of the verb depends on the subject that follows *There*.

> There *is* a *flaw* in Monique's design.

> There *are* several *flaws* in Monique's design.

ESL *focus* NONCOUNT NOUNS AND GERUNDS

Singular verbs are used with noncount nouns and gerunds.

NONCOUNT NOUN   The *information* is inaccurate.

GERUND   *Winning* is fun.

For more information about noncount nouns, see the ESL Focus in B1-a.

WHO, WHICH, THAT

Verbs in dependent clauses introduced by the relative pronouns *who, that,* and *which* must agree with the antecedents of these relative pronouns.

> The *Stoneys,* who *are* related to the Plains Assiniboine, traditionally lived along the foothills of the Rockies.

> The *language* that *is* native to the Stoneys is a dialect of the Dakota language spoken by the Sioux.

PLURAL FORM, SINGULAR MEANING

Some nouns ending in *-s* are singular in meaning and therefore take singular verbs.

> is
>
> *Mathematics* are an essential skill.

Some of these nouns may be either singular or plural depending on the context.

SINGULAR   Statistics *is* the most challenging course in the new curriculum.

PLURAL   His statistics *are* accurate.

In the singular example above, *statistics* denotes a field of study; in the plural example, it refers to a collection of specific information.

Words referred to as words or terms take singular verbs.

> is
>
> *Councillors* are a term that is gender-neutral.

PHRASES OF MEASURE AND QUALITY

Units of money, time, volume, mass, length, and distance take singular verbs.

> is
>
> Two kilometres are the equivalent of a mile and a quarter.

TITLES OF WORKS

The title of a book, film, or other work of art takes a singular verb even if the title has a plural or compound form.

> was
>
> Tomson Highway's *The Rez Sisters* were first produced at the Native Canadian Centre of Toronto in 1986.

G2-b   Tense Agreement

Verb tenses should clearly establish the time of the actions being described in a sentence or a passage. Tenses should be changed only when the context requires a shift.

The belief that Newfoundland *is* populated exclusively by

fishers *is* patently untrue. Yet this popular myth about

perpetuates

Newfoundlanders perpetuated itself.

Problems with tenses can occur when quotations are used to support commentary. A sentence that combines commentary and quotation can create an even more subtle problem.

AWKWARD   Dickens *observes* that Coke Town "*was* a
                 triumph of fact; it *had* no greater taint of
                 fancy in it than Mrs. Gradgrind." Dickens
                 had no admiration for industrial Britain.

You could eliminate the awkward shift in tenses in the first sentence by changing the tenses of the verbs in the quotation from past to present. When you alter a quotation in some way, you must enclose the added or changed words in brackets. (For information about brackets, see P8.)

REVISED   Dickens *observes* that Coke Town "[*is*] a
                 triumph of fact; it [*has*] no greater taint of
                 fancy in it than Mrs. Gradgrind." Dickens
                 has no admiration for industrial Britain.

NOTE: Changing verb tenses in a quotation is permissible only if the change does not substantially alter the meaning of the quotation.

G2-c Pronoun–Antecedent Agreement

Pronouns are words that replace nouns (see B1-b). A pronoun must agree with its antecedent—the word it replaces—in *number, gender,* and *person.*

The *soldiers* learned that *their* peacekeeping duties would be expanded.

COMPOUND ANTECEDENTS

When the parts of a compound antecedent are joined by *and,* the matching pronoun is plural.

Madonna and k.d. lang have forged *their* individual careers in remarkably different ways.

A compound antecedent that is preceded by *each* or *every* requires a singular pronoun.

Each car and truck must meet anti-smog standards before *it* is allowed on the road.

When a compound antecedent is joined by *or* or *nor*, the pronoun agrees with the nearest antecedent.

Neither *coach* nor *players* are happy about *their* new uniforms.

INDEFINITE PRONOUNS

When the antecedent is an indefinite pronoun whose meaning is singular, the matching pronoun is singular.

One of the hockey players lost *her* temper.

When the antecedent is an indefinite pronoun whose meaning is plural, the matching pronoun is plural.

Many of the teammates raised *their* arms in jubilation.

When the antecedent is an indefinite pronoun whose meaning can be singular or plural (e.g., *all, any, none,* and *some*), the matching pronoun is singular or plural depending on the noun it refers to.

SINGULAR   *Some* of the *art* appealed to *its* viewers.

PLURAL   *Some* of the *politicians* have broken *their* campaign promises.

Indefinite pronouns such as *one, anyone, someone, each, everybody, no one,* and *nobody* raise the problem of sexist bias when they are matched with a singular pronoun that is exclusionary and sexist.

EXCLUSIONARY   *Everybody* has to buy *his* own books.

To avoid exclusion, you can use both masculine and feminine pronouns.

REVISED   *Everyone* has to buy *his* or *her* own books.

Alternatively, you can replace the indefinite pronoun with a plural noun.

REVISED   *Students* have to buy *their* own books.

See U3 for a more detailed discussion of inclusive language.

ESL *focus* GENDER AND AGREEMENT

The gender of nouns and pronouns varies from language to language and from culture to culture. The two major languages in Canada, French and English, use gender in quite different ways. In French, pronouns and the nouns they replace are either masculine or feminine. In English, most of these constructions are gender-neutral.

- The *cat* rolled on *its* back.
- The *tree* shaded the cat with *its* branches.

Nouns that are gender-specific include *bull*, *cow*, *stag*, *doe*, *gander*, *goose*, *lady*, *lord*, *prince*, *princess*, *man*, and *woman*.

G2-d Person Agreement

Do not shift among first, second, and third person unless meaning demands it. The following passage illustrates awkward and unnecessary shifts in person:

AWKWARD   If *people* go to a movie theatre on the
           weekend, *they* will probably encounter
           large lineups for the most popular films. *I*
           may even end up going to a film *I* did not
           intend, or want, to see. To ensure that *you*
           see the film of your choice, *you* should
           arrive early.

In the passage, the writer shifts from the third-person noun and pronoun (*people/they*), to the first-person pronoun (*I*), to the second-person pronoun (*you*). The problems of clarity and logic are easily solved by eliminating the person agreement problems. Replace the italicized pronouns with "you" and there are no longer unnecessary shifts in person.

G3 Common Sentence Problems

G3-a Unclear Pronoun Reference

Pronouns that do not refer clearly to their antecedents are common sources of confusion for readers. A pronoun reference is ambiguous when the pronoun could refer to more than one antecedent.

AMBIGUOUS   Roger told Samarjit that he was being
             transferred to Montreal.

As the following revisions indicate, there are two possible interpretations for this sentence.

CLEAR   Roger told Samarjit, "You are being transferred to Montreal."

CLEAR   Roger told Samarjit, "I am being transferred to Montreal."

Another kind of unclear pronoun reference occurs when there are too many intervening words between a pronoun and its antecedent.

CONFUSING   Economic recessions are the result of a multitude of factors that, in isolation, may be harmless; it is the confluence of these factors that triggers *them*.

A reader of this passage would have difficulty making the connection between the pronoun *them* and its antecedent *recessions*. To clarify, you could eliminate the pronoun by combining the two sentences.

CLEAR   Economic recessions are triggered by a confluence of factors that, in isolation, may be harmless.

The use of *it, this, that,* or *which* as a pronoun reference is another source of potential confusion. The problem arises when these pronouns are used to refer to whole sentences or ideas rather than to specific antecedents.

VAGUE   Each year during the holiday season, hundreds of bikers organize a drive to collect toys for disadvantaged children. They deposit the toys at a local donation centre on December 15. *This* is an unexpected and pleasing phenomenon.

In the preceding example, it is not clear what *This* refers to— the organized toy drive, the depositing of the toys at the donation centre, or perhaps both activities. To avoid confusion, you could revise so that *This* is eliminated.

G3-b Misplaced Modifiers

A misplaced modifier is a word, phrase, or clause that does not point clearly to the word or words it is intended to modify.

MISPLACED   Violence is a growing problem in modern society *which stems from fear and ignorance.*

In the preceding example, the dependent clause *which stems from fear and ignorance* follows *society* and therefore appears to modify it.

REVISED   Violence, *which stems from fear and ignorance,* is a growing problem in modern society.

In general, a modifier should be placed either right before or right after the word or words it modifies.

Limiting modifiers such as *only, even, exactly, almost, nearly, hardly,* and *just* should be placed right before the words they modify. Note how changing the position of the limiting modifier alters the meaning of each of the following examples.

Only Ann Marie will receive $200 from her aunt.

Ann Marie will receive *only* $200 from her aunt.

Ann Marie will receive $200 from her *only* aunt.

A *squinting modifier* is a modifier that could refer to either the word(s) before it or the word(s) after it.

SQUINTING   Sonny said *in the morning* he would look for the missing dog.

You could avoid such ambiguity by revising the sentence in either of the following ways.

REVISED   *In the morning,* Sonny said he would look for the missing dog.

REVISED   Sonny said he would look for the missing dog *in the morning.*

G3-c   Dangling Modifiers

Dangling modifiers are words, phrases, or clauses that refer to something that is absent from the sentence. Frequently positioned at the beginnings of sentences, they appear to modify words they were never intended to modify. To revise a dangling modifier, you need to name the actor to which it properly refers.

DANGLING   While hiking in the desert, a mirage appeared in the distance. [A mirage cannot hike.]

REVISED   While hiking in the desert, *I* saw a mirage appear in the distance.

PASSIVE VOICE AND DANGLING MODIFIERS

PASSIVE/
DANGLING
           ┌───── SUBJECT ─
Having lost patience, the malfunctioning

┌──────┐┌─VERB ─┐
computer was replaced.

Restoring the agent of the action by shifting the sentence to active voice removes the dangling element.

              ┌SUBJECT┐┌VERB┐
ACTIVE   Having lost patience, the student replaced

┌────── OBJECT────────┐
the malfunctioning computer.

For more information about the passive voice, see U5.

G3-d Faulty Parallel Structure

When Shakespeare has Hamlet say "*To die, to sleep, to sleep,* / perchance *to dream*" (3.1.64–65), he is using parallel structure. Parallelism refers to a series of like grammatical elements—words, phrases, or clauses—that are expressed in repeating grammatical constructions.

WORDS   *Running, walking,* and *cycling* are all good forms of exercise.

PHRASES   To get to the market, you walk *across the street, through the park,* and *into the square.*

CLAUSES   To run for office, *you may have to join a party;* to join a party, *you may have to modify your controversial views.* [This example also includes parallel phrases—*to run for office, to join a party.*]

You violate parallel structure when you fail to use the same grammatical form for elements in a series.

NONPARALLEL   An effective leader is capable of inspiring loyalty, taking risks, and the acceptance of responsibility.

PARALLEL   An effective leader is capable of *inspiring loyalty, taking risks,* and *accepting responsibility.*

For more information about parallel structure, see C4-c and S5-c.

WORD CHOICE AND SPELLING

W1 Diction

W1-a Redundancy and Wordiness

A wordy sentence is one that contains more words than are necessary to convey the meaning of the sentence. For example, a sentence may contain a nonessential phrase such as *In my opinion* or a redundant phrase such as *at the present time* (when *now* would suffice).

WORDY   In my opinion, I believe that we have never had it better than we do right now in the early years of the twenty-first century.

REVISED   We have never had it better than we do now.

Combining sentence elements is one of the means by which you can achieve economy in your writing (see S-5a). A process that can help you identify redundancies is the proofreading sweep (see F5-d).

W1-b Appropriate Connotations

Denotation is the exact, literal meaning of a word—the kind of meaning expressed in a dictionary definition. *Connotation* refers to the values and associations attached to a word. For example, the word *home* denotes "physical structure within which one lives" and connotes such things as "refuge," "sanctuary," "haven," or "retreat." The connotations you select will depend on your context—specifically, your audience, purpose, and subject.

full-figured

Our new line of swimwear is ideal for overweight customers. [A retailer would not use the word *overweight* because it connotes obesity.]

W1-c Language Levels

Like speech, writing can be formal or informal. For example, *employer* and *They became angry* are formal; *boss* and *They got mad* are informal. The following statements about free trade provide a further illustration of the two language levels.

INFORMAL   Free trade is just a bunch of big shots who plan to get rich at our expense.

FORMAL   Free trade is one of the mechanisms by which powerful corporate interests exploit workers for personal gain.

The language level you use will depend on your purpose, audience, and subject. More personal than formal writing, informal writing is appropriate when your objective is to please or entertain. A greater degree of formality is appropriate for academic, business, and professional writing (reports, essays, and the like).

W1-d Specific and Concrete Diction

Much of the cumulative effect of your diction has to do with the extent to which you choose words that are (1) specific rather than general and (2) concrete rather than abstract. *General* words identify a class of things (*book*); *specific* words name a particular member of the class (*The Apprenticeship of Duddy Kravitz*). *Abstract* terms are words or phrases that refer to ideas or qualities (*justice, beauty*); *concrete* terms are words or phrases referring to things that exist in the material world (*court, painting*). Although general and abstract words are sometimes necessary to convey your meaning, specific and concrete words are usually preferable because they make your prose more vivid and precise. The following chart demonstrates the differences between the four types of words.

GENERAL	LESS GENERAL	SPECIFIC	MORE SPECIFIC
car	American car	Pontiac	Pontiac TransAm
tree	deciduous tree	willow	weeping willow
furniture	chair	armchair	recliner

ABSTRACT	LESS ABSTRACT	CONCRETE	MORE CONCRETE
entertainment	visual entertainment	film	horror film
thoroughfare	route	street	Yonge Street
covering	cloth protection	jacket	brown leather jacket

Readers hunger for specific information, specific examples, and specific words. Wherever you have a choice, use the specific and concrete word instead of the general and abstract alternative.

W1-e Clichés

Clichés are expressions that were once fresh but have become tired and predictable through overuse. Here are some examples:

Raw hamburger is something you should avoid *like the plague.*

The mayor's comments are nothing but *smoke and mirrors.*

We should *leave no stone unturned* in our search for truth.

If a cliché offers an efficient way of expressing something, do not be afraid to use it. Expressions such as *tongue in cheek* and *rule of thumb* are probably preferable to unwieldy, invented alternatives. Generally, however, you should use your proofreading sweep as an opportunity to replace clichés with original and exact phrasing.

W1-f   Jargon

Jargon is the specialized language of a profession or group. Academics, lawyers, and doctors, among others, use jargon to facilitate communication within their respective professions. The problem occurs when the jargon is used to communicate with a nonspecialist audience. Computer manuals, for example, are sometimes replete with acronyms or initialisms (abbreviations that commonly replace the words they stand for) that are incomprehensible to technologically challenged readers. How many of the following computer-related initialisms are you familiar with?

- PCMCIA slot
- LPTI
- USB connector
- IDE connector
- LAN connector
- HTML
- URL
- DNS
- ISP
- IEEE 1394

Use specialized language only if you are sure your audience will understand it. If you must use jargon in communicating with a nonspecialist audience, be sure to provide the necessary definitions.

W1-g   Idioms

An idiom is a phrase that is peculiar to a certain language. The fact that idioms do not follow standard rules and cannot be interpreted literally makes them especially challenging for ESL learners. Consider the statement *He is on top of the situation.* The idiom *on top of* would pose no difficulty for a native speaker, but it could very well mystify someone whose first language is not English.

Idiom often dictates which prepositions are used with which verbs. Here are some examples:

abide *by* (a decision)	in accordance *with*
abide *in* (a place or state)	independent *of*

according *to*
accuse *of*
angry *with*
averse *to*
capable *of*
comply *with*
die *of*
different *from*
identical *with/to*

inferior *to*
intend *to*
jealous *of*
preferable *to*
prior *to*
run *off* (not *off of*)
superior *to*
sure *of*
try *to*

ESL *focus* PREPOSITION USED TO INDICATE TIME AND PLACE

The following list demonstrates how to use *in, at,* and *on* to
indicate time and place.

TO INDICATE TIME

IN *Portion of time:* in the afternoon, in thirty seconds, in
ten minutes, in two hours, in three days, in a month,
in a year, in 1867, in January, in the spring

AT *Specific time:* at 8:35, at noon, at lunch, at the start
of the game

ON *Specific day:* on Monday, on my birthday, on July 1,
on St. Patrick's Day

TO INDICATE PLACE

IN *Enclosed area:* in the box, in the shower, in the living
room, in the tunnel

Location: in the street, in Hamilton, in Ontario, in
Canada

AT *Location:* at the corner, at the store, at the studio, at
the computer, at the table

ON *Surface:* on the page, on the book, on the table, on
Yonge Street, on the prairies

In English, some verbs are followed by different prepositions depending on the object of the preposition.

adapt *to* (a situation); adapt *from* (a source)
agree *with* (a person); agree *to* (terms); agree *on* (a plan)
compare *to* (something in a different group); compare *with*
(something in the same group)
conform *to*; conform *with*
differ *with* (a person); differ *over* (a question)

occupied *with* (a thing); occupied *by* (a person); occupied *in* (an act)

rewarded *by* (someone); rewarded *for* (something); rewarded *with* (an object)

wait *at* (a place); wait *for* (someone or something); wait *on* (a customer)

ESL*focus* PHRASAL VERBS

A special type of idiom is the phrasal verb, which consists of a verb followed by one or two prepositions (called *particles* in this context). One of the difficulties of phrasal verbs for ESL learners is that their meaning as a unit is distinct from the meaning of the parts considered individually. The meaning of *look out* in "Look out for falling debris" (where *look out* is a phrasal verb) is different from the meaning of *look out* in "Look out the window" (where *look out* are two independent words).

The following list of phrasal verbs does two things. First, it shows what preposition or adverb goes with the verb to make the phrasal verb. Second, it uses an intervening pronoun to demonstrate whether a word may come between the verb and its particle—as in *take (her/it) out*.

ask (her) out	go out	put (it) back
break (it) down	go over	put (it) off
bring (her/it) out	grow up	put (it) on
burn (it) down/up	hand (it) in	put (it) out
call (her) up	hand (it) out	put (it) together
call (it) off	hang (it) up	put up
clean (it) up	hang on	quiet down
clean up	help (her) out	run across
come across	help out	run into
cut (it) up	keep on	run out
do (it) over	keep up	shut (it) off
drop (her/it) off	leave (it) out	speak up
drop in	look (it) over	stay away
drop out	look (it) up	stay up
fill (it) out	look into	take (her) out
fill (it) up	make (it) up	take (it) off
get along	pick (it) out	take (it) over
get away	pick (it/her) up	take care of
get up	play around	think (it) over
give (it) away	point (it) out	throw (it) away
give in	put (it) aside	throw (it) out
give up	put (it) away	try (it) on

(continued)

try (it) out	turn out	wake up
turn (it) down	turn up	wear out
turn (it) on	wake (her) up	wrap (it) up

W2 Using a Dictionary

A sample entry, taken from the *ITP Nelson Canadian Dictionary*, illustrates the various components of a dictionary entry.

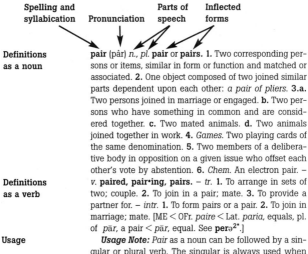

Spelling and syllabication **Pronunciation** **Parts of speech** **Inflected forms**

Definitions as a noun

pair (pår) *n., pl.* **pair** or **pairs. 1.** Two corresponding persons or items, similar in form or function and matched or associated. **2.** One object composed of two joined similar parts dependent upon each other: *a pair of pliers.* **3.a.** Two persons joined in marriage or engaged. **b.** Two persons who have something in common and are considered together. **c.** Two mated animals. **d.** Two animals joined together in work. **4.** *Games.* Two playing cards of the same denomination. **5.** Two members of a deliberative body in opposition on a given issue who offset each other's vote by abstention. **6.** *Chem.* An electron pair. –

Definitions as a verb

v. **paired, pair•ing, pairs.** – *tr.* **1.** To arrange in sets of two; couple. **2.** To join in a pair; mate. **3.** To provide a partner for. – *intr.* **1.** To form pairs or a pair. **2.** To join in marriage; mate. [ME < OFr. *paire* < Lat. *paria*, equals, pl. of *pār*, a pair < *pār*, equal. See **perə²*.**]

Usage

Usage Note: Pair as a noun can be followed by a singular or plural verb. The singular is always used when *pair* denotes the set taken as a single entity: *This pair of shoes is on sale.* A plural verb is used when the members are considered as individuals: *The pair are working together.* After a number other than one, *pair* can be either singular or plural, but the plural is now more common: *She bought six pairs (or pair) of stockings.*

W3 Spelling

W3-a Strategies for Improving Your Spelling

If you want to improve your spelling, you will have to find out what kinds of errors you commonly make. You can use your chart of spelling errors (described below) as a checklist of problems to look for when you are writing. Here are some methods you can use to improve your spelling:

1. With a handbook or a book devoted exclusively to spelling, learn the basic rules that govern the spellings of English words. You should at least learn the rules governing

    *   the spelling of words with *ie* or *ei* in them

    *   the addition of prefixes to existing words

    *   the addition of suffixes to existing words

    *   the doubling of a final consonant

    *   the formation of plural forms of words

    *   the spelling of possessives and contractions

    *   the differences among words employing *ceed, cede,* and *sede*

2. Make a list, in chart form, of the words you misspell. Divide your chart into two columns. Write down the misspelled word in the first column and the correct spelling in the second column. In the second column, make a note of any rule governing the correct spelling. List the words in your chart alphabetically and review the chart often. Typically, a writer's spelling errors have a pattern to them; you will discover your own pattern as you chart your spelling errors and determine the reasons for them.

3. Practise the spelling of new and difficult words. When you read a new chapter in one of your texts, list the new words you encounter and other words you find used in a way that is unique to that field of study. Use these newly acquired words in your writing until you can spell and use them correctly. With some subjects, it may even be worthwhile to maintain a running file of new words and their meanings.

4. Share your proofreading with another student. People sometimes have difficulty discovering a spelling error simply because they fail to recognize that the error is, in fact, an error. A second reader can pick up errors you missed. Another useful device for proofreading is to read your text backward. This forces you to focus on the words rather than the sentences and their cumulative meaning.

W3-b Homophones

Homophones are words that have the same sound—or nearly the same sound—but different spellings and meanings. Here are some homophones that are pronounced alike:

aid/aide	it's/its	stationary/
aloud/allowed	know/no	stationery
bear/bare	led/lead	there/their/they're
by/buy	lessen/lesson	two/too/to
coarse/course	miner/minor	weak/week
compliment/	past/passed	weather/whether
complement	piece/peace	where/wear/ware
council/counsel	principal/principle	which/witch
fourth/forth	rein/rain/reign	who's/whose
hear/here	right/rite/write	your/you're
heard/herd	sight/site/cite	

The homophones in the following list sound somewhat alike but have different meanings.

accept/except	illicit/elicit
advise/advice	immanent/eminent/imminent
affect/effect	later/latter
allusion/illusion	lose/loose
alter/altar	moral/morale
are/our	personal/personnel
ascent/assent	proceed/precede
dairy/diary	quit/quite
dessert/desert	sense/since
device/devise	then/than
envelop/envelope	through/thorough

Related to homophones are *homographs,* words that are identical in form but have different meanings. Some homographs have the same pronunciation (the noun *quail* and the verb *quail*; others do not (the verb *conduct* and the noun *conduct*). *Homonym* is the general term for words of different meaning that are spelled or pronounced the same. If you are not sure of the distinctions between these words, consult your dictionary for their meanings.

ESL *focus* HOMOPHONES: POSSESSION AND

CONTRACTION

The homophones *its/it's, your/you're, whose/who's,* and *their/they're* can be particularly troublesome for ESL learners. You will be able to distinguish between these homophones if you remember that an apostrophe in a homophone marks a contraction, while the absence of such an apostrophe indicates possession.

> *It's* none of her business. [contraction of *it is*]

> The team has lost *its* competitive spirit. [possessive form of *it*]

> *Who's* participating in the debate? [contraction of *who is*]

> *Whose* book is that? [possessive form of *who*]

W3-c   Canadian Spelling

Canadian spelling is a blend of American and British spellings. The following list shows the preferred spellings of some common words in an American dictionary (*Merriam-Webster's Collegiate Dictionary,* 10th ed.), a British dictionary (*The Concise Oxford Dictionary,* 10th ed.), and three Canadian dictionaries—the *ITP Nelson Canadian Dictionary of the English Language,* the *Gage Canadian Dictionary,* and *The Canadian Oxford Dictionary.*

You should abide by the spelling preferences of your chosen dictionary throughout any given writing assignment.

AMERICAN	BRITISH	CANADIAN
airplane	aeroplane	airplane
anemia	anaemia	anemia
ax	axe	axe
catalog	catalogue	catalogue
center, theater	centre, theatre	centre, theatre
check	cheque	cheque
color, humor	colour, humour	colour, humour
defense, offense	defence, offence	defence, offence
gray	grey	grey
hemorrhage	haemorrhage	hemorrhage
inquire	enquire	inquire
judgment	judgement	judgment
maneuver	manoeuvre	manoeuvre
mold	mould	mould
pajamas	pyjamas	pyjamas

(continued)

AMERICAN	BRITISH	CANADIAN
pediatric	paediatric	pediatric
practice (n. and v.)	practice (n.), practise (v.)	practice (n.), practise (v.)
program	programme	program
referenda	referendums	referendums
sizable	sizeable	sizable
traveler	traveller	traveller

W3-d Spell Checkers

The spell checker, a standard feature of word processors, allows you to check your document's spelling and grammar. Many writers have found that this word-processing tool is of limited use. A spell checker does not alert you to certain typographical errors (such as *causal* when you mean to say *casual*) or to your own errors in grammar (such as *they're* when the grammatically correct word is *their*).

For Canadian writers, the spell checker has another drawback. The dictionaries in most spell checkers are American. If you use Canadian spelling in your documents, you must build a customized dictionary so that the spell checker does not reject such Canadian/British spellings as *colour* and *traveller*.

U

USAGE ISSUES

U1 Pronoun Case

There are three cases in English: the *subjective* case, which is used for the subject of the sentence; the *objective* case, which shows the recipient of the action of the verb or preposition; and the *possessive* case, which indicates ownership. The pronoun forms for each of the three cases are listed below.

SUBJECTIVE CASE	OBJECTIVE CASE	POSSESSIVE CASE
I	me	my
we	us	our
you	you	your
he, she	him, her	his, her
it, one	it, one	its, one's
they	them	their

Seven common problems writers have in dealing with pronoun case are discussed below. For more information about pronoun case, see B1–b.

U1-a *I* or *Me*

Some writers have difficulty deciding whether to use *I* or *me* in a sentence. You can avoid confusion by remembering that *I* functions as a subject, while *me* functions as an object of a verb or preposition.

SUBJECT	*I* like the mild winters in Vancouver.
OBJECT OF VERB	The mild winters in Vancouver surprised *me*.
OBJECT OF PREPOSITION	The mild winters in Vancouver appealed to *me*.

U1-b Appositives

A pronoun that is used as an appositive (B2–b) appears in the case of the noun it renames.

I
Two contestants, Ellen and me, arrived early. [The appositive *Ellen and I* renames the subject *contestants*.]

The organizers congratulated the victorious teammates,
me
Will, Diego, and I. [The appositive *Will, Diego, and me* renames the direct object *teammates*.]

U1-c *We* or *Us*

When the pronouns *we* or *us* are used with a noun, the case of the pronoun depends on whether the noun functions as a subject or an object.

We
Us Manitobans are proud of our ethnically diverse culture. [*Manitobans* is the subject.]

us
Parks Canada awarded we volunteers with a trip to Pukashwa National Park. [*Volunteers* is the object of a preposition.]

U1-d Pronouns with *Than* or *As*

Using pronouns in comparisons beginning with *than* or *as* can be tricky. By mentally completing the sentence, you can determine which pronoun is appropriate.

I
Fazil is taller than me. (am)

him
The voters distrusted no other politician as much as he.

Changing the pronoun case in comparisons with *than* or *as* radically alters the meaning of the sentence.

SUBJECTIVE CASE   Jean-Paul loves Maria more than *I*.
                  [Jean-Paul loves Maria more than I do.]

OBJECTIVE CASE   Jean-Paul loves Maria more than *me*.
                  [Jean-Paul loves Maria more than he loves me.]

U1-e Pronouns with Infinitives

Pronouns that function as either the subject or object of an infinitive (the base form of the verb preceded by *to*) must appear in the objective case.

SUBJECT OF INFINITIVE   He wanted *me* to see the play.

OBJECT OF INFINITIVE   He wanted to take *me* to the play.

87

U1-f   Pronouns with Gerunds and Present Participles

Pronouns that modify gerunds (verbals ending in *-ing* that function as nouns) or gerund phrases (a gerund with any modifier, object, or complement) appear in the ~~objective~~ case.

possessive

our
The odds against us winning the lottery are ridiculously high. [*Our* modifies the gerund phrase *winning the lottery*.]

For more information about gerunds and other verbals, see B2-b and the ESL Focus entitled "Gerunds and Infinitives after Verbs" in B1-c.

U1-g   Pronouns as Subject Complements

Pronouns that function as subject complements—words that follow linking verbs (B1-c) and identify or describe the subject—always appear in the subjective case.

she
It is her who approved the loan.

U2   Pronoun Choice

U2-a   *Who* or *Whom*

Who and *whom* may be relative pronouns that introduce dependent clauses (B2-d) or interrogative pronouns (B1-b) that introduce questions. In formal written English, the grammatical rule is straightforward. Use *who* (or *whoever*) when the pronoun is a subject or a subject complement. Use *whom* (or *whomever*) when the pronoun is the direct or indirect object of a verb or the object of a preposition.

The man *who* had been arrested called his lawyer. [relative pronoun as subject of the clause *who had been arrested*]

The foundation grants scholarships to *whomever* it wants. [relative pronoun as object of the preposition *to*]

Who won the lacrosse game last night? [interrogative pronoun as subject]

ı sitting? [interrogative pronoun as
sition *with*]

hich

relative pronouns introduce adjective
clauses. Adjective clauses modify nouns or pronouns and may
be restrictive or nonrestrictive. *That* is used to introduce a
restrictive, or essential, clause. A restrictive clause limits the
meaning of the noun it modifies and is essential to the
meaning of the sentence. *Which* is used to introduce a nonrestrictive, or nonessential, clause. A nonrestrictive clause,
which is always set off by commas, merely adds information
and therefore can be removed without changing the basic
meaning of the sentence. (For more information about restrictive and nonrestrictive elements, see P1-b.)

RESTRICTIVE CLAUSE   The building *that* first caught
                            my eye was the CN Tower.

NONRESTRICTIVE CLAUSE   Metal roofing, *which* is
                            lightweight and inexpensive, is
                            not suitable for this climate.

U3 Inclusive Language

U3-a Ethnicity and Race

Language can demean or exclude individuals or groups on the
basis of ethnicity, race, and culture. For example, the word
Eskimo, which may have come from the Abenaki word
esquimantsic or the Chippewa word *ashkimequ* (meaning
eaters of raw meat), has a pejorative connotation for Inuit
people. Similarly, dividing the Canadian population into ethnic
groups such as *Chinese-Canadians* or *Indo-Canadians* can
exclude people from the mainstream. (Of course, it would be
necessary to make such distinctions if you were writing about
the cultures of Canada from a historical or sociological point of
view.)

U3-b Gender

Sexist language also serves to exclude members of your audience. This kind of exclusionary language can reflect stereo-
typical thinking, such as the assumption that all nurses are

89

women. A more concrete expression of sexist language is the traditional use of the generic personal pronoun *he*.

EXCLUSIONARY   When a student enters college, *he* has to buy *his* own textbooks.

One solution to the generic *he* is to use a construction such as *she or he* or *she/him*. However, as the following revision indicates, awkwardness can result if the usage is excessive.

AWKWARD   When a student enters college, *he/she* has to buy *his/her* own textbooks.

A preferable solution in this instance is to make the pronouns and their antecedent plural.

INCLUSIVE   When *students* enter college, *they* have to buy *their* own textbooks.

In some cases, you can address the problem of sexist language by substituting a gender-neutral term for a sexist term.

EXCLUSIONARY   The *chairman* is convening a meeting.

INCLUSIVE   The *chairperson* is convening a meeting.

To avoid gender bias in your writing, refer to the following list of sexist terms and possible gender-inclusive replacements.

EXCLUSIONARY	INCLUSIVE
alderman	councillor
chairman	chairperson, chair, moderator
fireman	firefighter
fisherman	fisher, angler
foreman	supervisor
mailman	postal worker, mail carrier
man	person, individual
mankind	human beings, humankind, human race, people
manpower	personnel, human resources
policeman	police, police officer
salesman	clerk, salesclerk, salesperson
steward, stewardess	flight attendant
to man	to operate, to staff

U4 Comparatives and Superlatives

All adjectives and adverbs have a base form (*hard, slowly*). In addition to their base form, most adjectives and adverbs have a comparative form (*harder, more slowly*) and a superlative form (*hardest, most slowly*). The comparative form is used to compare two things, while the superlative form is used to compare three or more things. (See also B1–d.)

U4-a Absolute Terms

Absolute terms such as *equal, fatal, perfect, square,* and *unique* should not be given a comparative or superlative form. You cannot describe something as *more unique* or *most unique,* for example, because there cannot be degrees of uniqueness.

U5 Active and Passive Voice

The voice of a verb depends on whether the subject of the sentence is acting or being acted upon. In the active voice, the subject *does* the action; in the passive voice, the subject *receives* the action.

ACTIVE   The governor general *dissolved* Parliament.

PASSIVE   Parliament *was dissolved* by the governor general.

Writers are generally advised to use the active voice as much as possible because it results in prose that is not only crisper and clearer, but more dynamic.

 The use of the passive voice is appropriate if the doer of the action is unknown or less important than the recipient of the action.

> In 1918, Canadian women *were given* the right to vote in federal elections. [doer less important than recipient]

U6 Split Infinitives

An infinitive consists of the base form of a verb preceded by *to* (*to walk, to believe, to represent*). A split infinitive occurs when the two parts of the infinitive are separated by a modifier consisting of a word, phrase, or clause (*to fervently believe*). A split infinitive that is awkward or potentially confusing to the reader should be eliminated.

AWKWARD   The politician was reluctant *to* forcefully
                 speak out in opposition to welfare reform.

REVISED   The politician was reluctant *to speak out*
                 forcefully in opposition to welfare reform.

Although the split infinitive is still frowned on by some authorities, it is not an error. In some instances, a split infinitive is preferable to an awkward alternative construction. *Few observers expect the Liberal candidate to actually lose* sounds better than *Few observers expect the Liberal candidate actually to lose* or *Few observers expect the Liberal candidate to lose actually*.

PUNCTUATION

P1 The Comma

Comma usage falls into two major divisions: commas used to *separate* and commas used to *set off.*

P1-a Commas to Separate

1. Use a comma before a coordinating conjunction (*and, but, yet, so, or, nor, for*) joining independent clauses.

    > Canadian history is replete with examples of federal–provincial conflict, so the recent wrangling about transfer payments is hardly surprising.

2. Use commas to separate three or more items—words, phrases, or clauses—in a series.

    > Carrots, beets, turnips, and potatoes were common winter vegetables in nineteenth-century Canada.

    > When he is happy, when he eats well, and when he is paid well, Pavarotti sings like an angel.

    Although some writers prefer to omit the comma separating the last two items, most authorities recommend that this final comma—called a *series* or *serial comma*—be retained to avoid confusion.

3. Use commas with dates, addresses, and titles. Note the absence of the comma before the postal code in the address example.

    > On September 12, 1994, Quebecers went to the polls to elect a new government.

    > Send the parcel to 2345 Willowbrook Crescent, Langley, British Columbia V3B 2K4.

P1-b Commas to Set Off

1. Use commas to set off introductory elements.

Unfortunately, many born politicians never enter politics.
[adverb]

The vocalist is hopeless; *however,* the new dancer shows promise. [conjunctive adverb]

When the contestants are ready, the game can begin.
[adverb clause]

Before the election, the candidates promised voters more than they could ever hope to deliver.
[prepositional phrase]

2. Use commas to set off nonrestrictive elements. An element is nonrestrictive if it adds information not essential to the meaning of the sentence; an element is restrictive if it defines or limits the noun in a way that is essential to the meaning of the sentence. (For more information about restrictive and nonrestrictive elements, see U2-b.)

    Atom Egoyan's *The Sweet Hereafter, which received co-production assistance from Toronto-based Alliance Atlantis,* is based on a Russell Banks short story. [nonrestrictive adjective clause]

    The stock market, *despite its risks,* has become the bedrock of retirement planning for many Canadians. [nonrestrictive prepositional phrase]

    The late Matt Cohen's final novel, *Elizabeth and After,* was the winner of the 1999 Governor General's Literary Award for fiction. [nonrestrictive appositive]

3. Use commas to set off transitional expressions, parenthetical expressions, explanatory terms, and contrasted elements.

    Whole wheat and vegetable oils, *for example,* are

rich in Vitamin E. [transitional expression]

Health care, *so far as I am concerned,* is an important issue. [parenthetical expression]

Nurture, *not nature,* is the leading cause of criminal behaviour. [contrasted element]

4. Use commas to set off forms of direct address, interrogative tags, the words *yes* and *no,* and mild interjections.

Ladies and gentlemen, kindly take your seats. [direct address]

You liked the film, *didn't you*? [interrogative tag]

Yes, it is raining. [word *yes*]

P1-c   Misuses of the Comma

Do *not* use a comma in the following situations.

1. To set off restrictive elements

   The team/ *that wins this game*/ will proceed to the finals.

2. Between a verb and its subject or object

   The governor of the Bank of Canada observed/ that the Canadian dollar is undervalued.

3. After the last item in a series

   Political parties are always looking for talented, articulate, and ambitious/ people to run for office.

4. Between cumulative adjectives

   He is a dear/ old/ man.

5. Before or after a coordinating conjunction joining compound elements

   She worked for a newspaper / and trained as a lawyer before entering politics.

6. With a question mark or an exclamation mark

    "Watch out!"/ James shouted.

7. To set off an indirect quotation

    Sir Wilfrid Laurier forecast/ that the twentieth century would belong to Canada.

P2   The Semicolon

1. Use a semicolon to link closely related independent clauses.

    The magazine article is not based on facts; it is
    ^
    based on rumour and speculation.

2. Use a semicolon to link a sentence introduced by a transitional expression (C4–a) to the previous sentence.

    Reva has a reputation for diligence; indeed, her
    ^
    coworkers describe her as a perfectionist.

3. Use semicolons to separate items in a series when one or more of the items has internal punctuation.

    The unlikely high-school clique consists of Mai, who

    loves to party; Samantha, who loves to study; and
    ^   ^
    Dave, who loves to sleep.

P3   The Colon

1. Use a colon after an independent clause to introduce a *list*, a *quotation*, an *appositive*, or an *explanation*.

    Visitors to foreign countries require the following: a
    ^
    foreign-language phrase book, traveller's cheques,

    health insurance; and a desire to experience dif-
    .
    ferent cultures. [list]

The coach urged his struggling team to reflect on the immortal words of Yogi Berra: "It ain't over till it's over." [quotation]

Mark's hypochondria is a response to his greatest fear: infection. [appositive]

The reason for the company's success is plain: it is far more nimble than its competitors. [explanation]

2. Use a colon with the following:

HOURS, MINUTES, AND SECONDS

time of day: 8:30 p.m.   elapsed time: 10:34:23.

SALUTATIONS IN LETTERS

Dear Sir or Madam:

ATTENTION/SUBJECT LINES IN LETTERS

Attention: Kulwinder Singh

COPY NOTATIONS IN LETTERS

C: Thomas Ruffini

ELEMENTS IN MEMO HEADINGS

To: Sylvie Campeau

From: Heather Thomas

Date: April 2, 2001

Subject: Year-end report

TITLES AND SUBTITLES

Shadow Maker: The Life of Gwendolyn MacEwen

BIBLICAL CHAPTERS AND VERSES

Matthew 6:28

PARTS OF BIBLIOGRAPHICAL ENTRIES

Seth, Vikram. *An Equal Music.* Toronto: McArthur & Company, 1999.

P4   Quotation Marks

P4-a   Direct Speech

1. Place double quotation marks around direct speech. Do not use quotation marks for *indirect speech* or for speech that is reported or paraphrased.

   > She said, "I'll meet you at the restaurant." [direct speech]

   > She said she would meet us at the restaurant. [indirect speech]

2. Use commas to set off speaker tags from quotations.

   > "The true character of the historical Grace Marks," writes Atwood, "remains an enigma."

   > EXCEPTION: Omit the comma when the speaker tag follows a quotation that ends with a question mark or an exclamation mark.

   > "Are you ready to go?" he asked.

3. Use single quotation marks to enclose quotations within quotations.

   > Alan Hustak's book *Titanic: The Canadian Story* tells of a British passenger, a woman named Esther Hart, who had a premonition of disaster. As Hart's daughter later recalled, "When she saw a headline in a newspaper that their new ship was unsinkable, she said, 'Now I know why I am frightened. This is flying in the face of God.'"

P4-b   Short and Long Quotations

1. Use quotation marks to enclose a prose quotation of fewer than five typed lines (MLA style) or forty words (APA style) in your essay.

   > Carol Shields has characterized Susanna Moodie as "a Crusoe baffled by her own heated imagination."

   When the prose quotation runs longer than four typed lines (MLA style) or is forty words or more (APA style), set it off from the text by indenting ten spaces (MLA) or five spaces (APA) from the left margin.

Quotations presented in this format, called a *block quotation,* are not enclosed in quotation marks.

> In *The Great Lone Land,* William Francis Butler captures the immensity of the Canadian prairie, and the damage that Europeans did to it as they moved west across the country:
>
> > Hundreds of thousands of skeletons dot the short scant grass; and when fire had laid barer still the level surface, the bleached ribs and skulls of long-killed bison whiten far and near the dark burnt prairie. There is something unspeakably melancholy in the aspect of this portion of the North-west. [MLA style]

2. Use quotation marks to enclose a poetry quotation that runs no more than three lines. Note the use of slashes to indicate the separation of lines (see P6).

> In "Cypresses," D.H. Lawrence writes, "Evil, what is evil? / There is only one evil, to deny life."

A poetry quotation longer than three lines is set off line by line as a block quotation.

> The opening lines of "A Poison Tree" illustrate the deceptive simplicity of William Blake's language:
>
> > I was angry with my friend:
> >
> > I told my wrath, my wrath did end.
> >
> > I was angry with my foe:
> >
> > I told it not, my wrath did grow.

P4-c Titles

Use quotation marks to enclose the titles of essays and articles, short stories, poems, songs, speeches, parts of books, and episodes of radio and television programs.

This poem invites, and suffers from, comparison with Sylvia Plath's searing "Daddy." [poem]

What do you think of Our Lady Peace's song "Superman's Dead"? [song]

The authors of this computer guide discuss everything from mice to modems in a chapter entitled "Inside Out." [part of a book]

In "Escape Clause," my favourite episode of *The Twilight Zone*, a man makes a deal with the devil in order to obtain immortality. [television program]

P4-d Other Uses for Quotation Marks

1. Quotation marks are sometimes used to set off words used ironically.

    My "assets" consist of an Ikea bedroom suite and an overdrawn bank account.

2. Quotation marks may be used to enclose words used as words or terms.

    The plural of "datum" is "data."

    NOTE: Italics may be used instead of quotation marks for this purpose (see M1–b).

3. Use quotation marks for words coined (invented) by a writer.

    Miller interviewed what he called "sexperts."

P4-e Quotation Marks with Other Punctuation

1. Place commas and periods *inside* closing quotation marks.

    "I'm studying for the chemistry exam," said Ahmed. "I expect to be up all night."

2. Place colons and semicolons *outside* quotation marks.

    The narrator's intellectual curiosity about his mother's disease evolves into "lunatic devotion"; he neglects his family to stay at his mother's side.

    Here is the terrible truth about the "anorexia industry": it reinforces the very phenomenon it is designed to combat.

3. Put question marks and exclamation marks inside quotation marks if they belong to the quotation and outside if they apply to the sentence as a whole.

He said, "What's the matter?"

Has anyone in your class read the essay entitled "A Dialectic of Aural and Objective Correlatives"?

4. Place footnote numbers and page citations outside quotation marks.

> As Abraham Maslow comments in his book *Motivation and Personality,* "It is quite true that man lives by bread alone when there is no bread."[1]

> In *The Intelligence of Dogs,* Stanley Coren describes the Dandie Dinmont terrier as "a very distinctive little dog with deep soulful eyes" (13).

P5   The Apostrophe

The apostrophe has three main uses: to indicate the possessive case; to substitute for letters in contractions; and to form the plural of letters, numbers, and words used as words or terms.

P5-a   Possession

1. Add an apostrophe and *-s* (*-'s*) to form the possessive case of singular nouns (including those ending in *-s*) and indefinite pronouns.

> The *teacher's* new car is a lemon.

> The *witness's* testimony is full of contradictions.

> The reading list includes *Dickens's Great Expectations.*

2. Add an apostrophe to form the possessive case of plural nouns ending in *-s.* If the plural does not end in *-s,* add an apostrophe and *-s* (*-'s*).

> The *Joneses'* house has been sold.

> The *women's* objectives have not been met.

3. To indicate joint possession by two or more owners, make only the last noun possessive. To indicate individual possession, make all nouns possessive.

> *Nova and Seb's* presentation was the most polished.

> *Candace's* and *Todd's* political views differ greatly.

4. To form the possessive of compound nouns (a noun consisting of two or more words), add –s to the last word.

> *Revenue Canada's* tax returns seem to get more complicated with each passing year.

P5-b Contractions

Contractions are formed when certain letters are left out of words or phrases. As the following examples illustrate, an apostrophe is used to replace the missing letter or letters:

cannot/can't	she is, she's
does not/doesn't	there is, there has/there's
I am/I'm	was not/wasn't
is not/isn't	who is/who's
it is/it's	would not/wouldn't

Contractions are used frequently in conversation and informal writing, but they are usually avoided in formal writing.

P5-c Plurals

Use apostrophes to form the plural of letters, numbers, and words used as words.

Remember to dot your *i's* and cross your *t's*. [letters]

The judges awarded Canadian pairs skaters Salé and Pelletier *6.0's* for their program. [number]

The two *Incomplete's* on Tim's transcript were a direct result of his illness earlier that year. [word used as word]

NOTE: The plural of abbreviations and dates can be formed with or without the apostrophe (YWCAs/YWCA's, 1990s/1990's). The current trend is to omit the apostrophe.

P6 The Slash

1. In a short quotation, use the slash, or solidus, to separate lines of a poem included within your text. Leave a space before and after each slash.

> In "Low Tide on Grand Pre," Bliss Carman describes the aging process: "I deemed / That time was ripe, and years had done / Their wheeling underneath the sun."

2. Use a slash to separate the numerator and denominator in a fraction and the elements of an abbreviated date. Do not include a space before and after the slash in these situations.

$$x/a + y/b = 1. \qquad\qquad 99/08/25$$

3. A slash is sometimes used instead of a hyphen to indicate a period overlapping two calendar years (2001/2) and to separate paired terms such as *student/teacher* and *producer/director*.

P7 Parentheses

1. Use parentheses to enclose supplementary information.

   Nellie McClung (1873–1951) fought for women's suffrage, factory safety legislation, and other reforms.

2. The material enclosed by parentheses may, among other things, identify, amplify, clarify, or comment.

   A study of Ottawa politics would necessarily focus on the three P's (power, perks, and patronage). [identifies]

   Genetic (hereditary) information is organized into threadlike structures called chromosomes. [clarifies]

3. Parentheses are also used to enclose numbers or letters in a list.

   To conduct the experiment, you require the following materials: (1) safety goggles, (2) electrolysis apparatus, (3) water, (4) 5 g sodium sulfate.

P8 Brackets

1. Use square brackets to enclose words or comments you have inserted into a quotation.

   Frank Newell "unexpectedly found [among the *Titanic*'s recovered dead] the body of a relative."

   Timothy Findley described Glenn Gould as one of the "god-people, [who] are the truly, absolutely gifted, almost beyond human dimension."

The second of the preceding example sentences shows how brackets can be used to make a quotation grammatically consistent with the rest of the sentence.

2. If there is an error in the quotation, you can follow the error with a bracketed *sic*. Latin for "so" or "thus," *sic* is a way of telling readers that the mistake was in the original.

> The CEO said the company would "do everything possible to exacerbate [*sic*] the strikers' demands."

P9 The Dash

1. Like commas or parentheses, dashes may set off parenthetical material. Dashes bring more emphasis to such material than either commas or parentheses.

> As the narrative shifts backward and forward in time, the suspense—and the reader's sense of dread—escalates to an almost unbearable pitch.

2. Like colons, dashes may be used to introduce a list, an appositive, or an explanation.

> The alternative bookstore offers seminars on three New Age topics—holistic medicine, Gaia theory, and reincarnation. [list]

> David Cronenberg explores his twin passions—science and literature—in his films. [appositive]

3. A dash may also be used to signal an interruption or an abrupt shift in tone or thought.

> "I don't understand what—" She broke off in confusion.

4. In MLA-style essays, you can use either two hyphens (--) or a word-processing dash (—) to form a dash. In APA-style essays, two hyphens (--) are used to indicate a dash. In both MLA and APA styles, there is no space before, between, or after the hyphens.

P10 Ellipses

1. The omission of words from a quotation is indicated by the use of ellipsis dots. Use three dots to indicate the omission of words within a sentence or the omission of a complete sentence or more within a quotation. (To

indicate an omission that is preceded by a complete sentence, use four dots, the first of which functions as a sentence period.)

> In their introduction to the *ITP Nelson Canadian Dictionary*, the authors write, "We have . . . sought to show how the development of . . . Canadian English . . . mirrors our development as a nation."

Here is the original text of the quotation in the above example (omissions in italics):

> We have *also* sought to show how the development of *our own variety of English,* Canadian English, mirrors our development as a nation.

When using MLA style (see D2), place square brackets arround the ellipsis dots that you add, to distinguish them from those in the original passage.

> Canada, to the anti-confederates, was a vast and incomprehensible place, an ocean of concerns away. It was a pale, half-baked country—too large to make any sense and [. . .] too underpopulated to be of any importance (Macfarlane 21).

In MLA style, brackets are also used with an ellipsis at the end of a sentence.

> We knew the second step might be harder. [. . .] But if we could break this link between ads and editorial content, then we wanted good ads for "women's products" too (Steinem 253).

2. Do not use ellipsis dots at the beginning of a quotation.

3. The omission of one or more lines of poetry is indicated by a line of spaced dots running approximately the length of the preceding line. (In MLA style, the line of dots would be enclosed in brackets.)

> Turning and turning in the widening gyre
> The falcon cannot hear the falconer;
> Things fall apart; the centre cannot hold;
>
> . . . .
> Surely some revelation is at hand;
> Surely the Second Coming is at hand.
>
> – William Butler Yeats, "The Second Coming"

4. Ellipsis dots may mark a pause or hesitation.

> He said, "It's just . . . I mean, I'm not sure."

MECHANICS

M1 Underlining or Italics

M1-a Titles of Works

In word-processed documents, titles of complete works are italicized or underlined. (For information about the formats recommended by the Modern Language Association and the American Psychological Association, see pages 135 and 156, respectively). In handwritten or typed copy, underlining is used to indicate italics (<u>The English Patient</u>). Quotation marks are used for short poems and titles that are parts of complete works, such as essays and short stories (see P4-c).

BOOKS	<u>The Blind Assassin</u>
CHOREOGRAPHIC WORKS	Ballanchine's <u>Agon</u>
COMIC STRIPS	<u>Peanuts</u>
FILMS	<u>Pulp Fiction</u>
JOURNALS	<u>Canadian Literature</u>
LONG MUSICAL COMPOSITIONS	Handel's <u>Messiah</u>
LONG POEMS	<u>The Waste Land</u>
MAGAZINES	<u>Maclean's</u>
NEWSPAPERS	<u>The Globe and Mail</u>
PAMPHLETS	Paine's <u>Common Sense</u>
PLAYS	<u>Billy Bishop Goes to War</u>
RADIO PROGRAMS	<u>Morningside</u>
TELEVISION PROGRAMS	<u>Kids in the Hall</u>
WORKS OF VISUAL ART	Michelangelo's <u>David</u>

NOTE: Do not italicize or underline the titles of (1) sacred books, such as the Bible, the Talmud, or the Koran; (2) legal and political documents, such as Magna Carta, the Charter of Rights and Freedoms, the Criminal Code, or the Canadian Environmental Protection Act; and (3) software, such as Microsoft Word or WordPerfect.

M1-b Other Uses

1. Italicize or underline the names of aircraft, spacecraft, ships, and trains.

It was the flight of the space shuttle *Discovery* in 1992 that made Roberta Bondar the second Canadian astronaut in space.

NOTE: Do not use italics or underlining for vehicle types (Boeing 747, Avro CF-100 Canuck).

2. Italicize or underline foreign words and phrases.

NOTE: Do not italicize or underline foreign words that are frequently used by English speakers and thus are considered part of the English language (e.g., "ad infinitum," "bona fide," "habeas corpus," "noblesse oblige," "per capita," "tour de force," and "vice versa").

3. Use italics or underlining for the biological classifications of plants, animals, insects, and microorganisms. Note that the genus name but not the species name is capitalized, e.g., *Rosa acicularis.*

4. Italicize or underline words, letters, and numbers referred to as words.

Spell *committed* with two *m*'s and two *t*'s.

A circled *46* appeared at the top of his math test.

NOTE: Quotation marks may be used instead of italics or underlining for this purpose. (See P4-d.)

5. Italicize or underline the names of legal cases.

Bhinder v. Canadian National Railway

6. Italics or underlining may be used to create emphasis.

Antidepressants can actually *cause* depression.

M2 Capitalization

M2-a Sentence Capitals

1. The first word of a sentence is capitalized unless the sentence is contained within another sentence and enclosed in parentheses or dashes.

The author follows his introduction with a historical overview of the right wing in Canada (a decline in racist activity after the Second World War ended in a "virtual explosion" in the 1970s and 1980s) and detailed sections on the Canadian Nazi Party and the Edmund Burke Society.

2. A quoted complete sentence that is blended into the writer's sentence begins with a lowercase letter.

    George Orwell believed that "modern English, especially written English, is full of bad habits."

If the quoted complete sentence has a more remote syntactic relation to the rest of the sentence, the initial capital is retained.

    As George Orwell said, "Modern English, especially written English, is full of bad habits."

3. If a quoted sentence is interrupted by a speaker tag (*he said, she wrote*, etc.), do not capitalize the first word after the speaker tag.

    "After one of these storms," she said, "the sky looks like pink cotton candy."

M2-b Proper Nouns

1. Proper nouns name particular persons, places, and things. Common nouns name generic classes of persons, places, and things.

PROPER NOUNS	COMMON NOUNS
Judith Thompson	a playwright
Jupiter	a planet
Giller Prize	a book award

2. Capitalize all proper nouns and the adjectives derived from them. Do not capitalize common nouns unless they begin a sentence. The following categories of words are always capitalized:

    • personal names

    • days of the week and months of the year

    • official and popular names of geographic areas

    • official names of organizations

    • names of deities, religions, and religious writings

    • names of racial, linguistic, religious, and other groups of people

- names of civic holidays and holy days

- names of historical periods

- trade names

- names of specific aircraft, spacecraft, ships, and trains

- names of structures

- names of planets, stars, and other bodies in space

3. Capitalize titles of persons that directly precede a proper name. Do not capitalize titles used alone or following a proper name.

> Prime Minister Chrétien is meeting with the U.S. president next week.

> Jean Chrétien, the prime minister, is meeting with the U.S. president next week.

M3 Abbreviations

M3-a Titles of Persons

1. Academic, religious, political, and military titles are usually abbreviated when they directly precede a full name and spelled out when they precede a surname alone.

Gov. Gen. Adrienne Clarkson   Governor General Clarkson

2. A title that stands alone is not abbreviated.

> *professor*
> My English prof. says that "London" is a good poem.

3. Do not use a title before a name if another title follows the name. The title *Dr. Yetta Abramsky, Ph.D.* is redundant. Either *Dr. Yetta Abramsky* or *Yetta Abramsky, Ph.D.* would be acceptable.

M3-b Geographical Names

1. The names of countries are usually spelled out in running text. A common exception is U.S., which may appear in text as an adjective but not as a noun.

UNACCEPTABLE	Canada's largest trading partner is the U.S.
ACCEPTABLE	Many Canadians are troubled by our dependence on the U.S. economy.

2. In bibliographical citations, the names of provinces, territories, and states are abbreviated. Listed below are the abbreviations for provinces/territories and the two-letter abbreviations used by Canada Post.

	TRADITIONAL	CANADA POST
Alberta	Alta.	AB
British Columbia	B.C.	BC
Manitoba	Man.	MB
New Brunswick	N.B.	NB
Newfoundland	Nfld.	NF
Northwest Territories	N.W.T.	NT
Nova Scotia	N.S.	NS
Nunavut	—	NU
Ontario	Ont.	ON
Prince Edward Island	P.E.I.	PE
Quebec	Que. or P.Q.	QC
Saskatchewan	Sask.	SK
Yukon Territory	Y.T.	YT

M3-c Acronyms and Initialisms

1. *Acronyms* are abbreviations that can be pronounced as words (*PEN*, *NAFTA*, *RAM*). *Initialisms* are abbreviations that are pronounced letter by letter (*MP*, *RCMP*, *VHS*, *IBM*).

2. If you think your audience is unlikely to know what an acronym or initialism stands for, write the full name at the first use, followed by the acronym or initialism in parentheses; in subsequent mentions, use the acronym or initialism by itself.

3. Geographical initialisms may be written with or without periods (*U.K.* or *UK*, *U.S.* or *USA*).

M3-d Era Designations and Time of Day

1. The abbreviation A.D. precedes a date, and B.C. follows a date. Acceptable alternatives are B.C.E. and C.E.

A.D. 1000   *anno Domini* (in the year of our Lord)

1000 B.C.   before Christ

1000 B.C.E.   before the common era

C.E. 1000   common era

NOTE: The four era designations are often set in small caps with or without periods (A.D./AD).

2. The abbreviations A.M. and P.M. are acceptable only when used with figures.

6:45 A.M.   *ante meridiem* (before noon)

10:30 P.M.   *post meridiem* (after noon)

NOTE: A.M. and P.M. are often set in lowercase letters (a.m./p.m.) or in small caps (P.M.).

M4 Numbers

M4-a Spelling Out

1. Numbers that can be expressed in one or two words should be spelled out in formal writing. (In technical and business writing, figures are often preferred, although usage varies.) Use figures for numbers that require more than two words to spell out.

> My mutual fund's investment portfolio includes
> *forty-seven*
> holdings in 47 Canadian blue-chip companies.

> *894*
> Wayne Gretzky scored eight-hundred-and-ninety-
> four goals in the course of his NHL career.

EXCEPTIONS: (1) Related numbers should be expressed in the same style: *Mike Harris captured 59 out of 103 seats in the 1999 provincial election.* (2) To express sums of money in the millions or billions of dollars, you may use a combination of numbers and words accompanied by the dollar sign (*$15 billion*).

2. Do not begin a sentence with a figure, even when other numbers in the sentence are expressed in figures.

> *Five*
> 5 employees are responsible for processing between 80 and 120 application forms.

A sentence that begins with a long number can be revised to avoid awkwardness.

UNACCEPTABLE   175 people attended Bob and Lynn's wedding.

REVISED   Bob and Lynn's wedding was attended by 175 people.

M4-b Punctuation of Numbers

In traditional English style, commas are used to separate groups of three digits. In SI (Système international d'unités) style, a space is used to mark the separation. The traditional style is appropriate for academic and general-interest materials. SI usage is usually restricted to technical or scientific writing.

85,000 [traditional]   85 000 [SI]

M4-c Uses of Numbers

Except at the beginning of a sentence, numbers are appropriate in the following instances:

ADDRESSES   215 Pacific Avenue, Suite 1407

DATES   August 24, 2001 (or 24 August 2001)

DECIMALS, FRACTIONS   0.09, 3/4

DIVISIONS OF BOOKS   Chapter 8, Volume 2, page 63

DIVISIONS OF PLAYS   Act II, Scene iv (or Act 2, Scene 4), lines 5–13 (or, in MLA style, 2.4.5–13)

EXACT SUMS OF MONEY $4,829, $2.51

PERCENTAGES   78 percent

SCORES   a 6–5 victory

RATIOS   a ratio of 3 to 1, 2-to-1 odds

TIME OF DAY   9:20 A.M. (but four o'clock)

M4-d Symbols and Units of Measurement

Symbols (such as %, ¢, =, @, and #) and units of measurement (such as *cm*, *g*, *km*, *kg*, *L*, and *m*) are appropriate in tables but not in the body of an essay.

EXCEPTIONS: (1) The dollar sign is always used with figures (as in $38.75). (2) Symbols may be used to express temperature (18°C, 102°F).

M5 Hyphens

M5-a Compound Words

A compound word is a word made up of two or more words. Compound words are written as separate words, as single words, or with hyphens.

SEPARATE WORDS	free trade, hard disk
SINGLE WORD	makeup, textbook, freewriting
WITH HYPHENS	medium-sized, first-class

Following are some guidelines concerning the use of hyphens in compound words:

1. Use hyphens to connect the parts of compounds that function as adjectives (*well-known writer*, *six-year-old boy*, *large-scale project*).

2. Use a hyphen after the prefixes *all-*, *self-*, *ex-*, and *quasi-* (*all-inclusive dinner*). Do not, however, use a hyphen in the words *selfish*, *selfhood*, *selfless*, and *selfsame*.

3. Use a hyphen with prefixes that precede a capital or a figure (*non-Native*, *post-1945*).

4. Use hyphens to prevent readers from misunderstanding the relationship between adjectives and the words they modify. *Light blue coat*, for example, could mean either a blue coat that is light in terms of its weight or a coat that is light blue in colour. Adding a hyphen would clarify the latter meaning (*light-blue coat*).

5. Use a hyphen in spelled-out fractions and in number compounds from twenty-one to ninety-nine (*fifty-two*, *one-seventh*).

6. A hyphen may be used to separate paired terms (*author-critic, parent-child, French-English*). A slash may also be used for this purpose. (See P6.)

7. Use a hyphen to separate identical vowels or consonants in some compounds, such as *anti-inflation, de-emphasize, bell-like*.

8. Use a hyphen to distinguish between such words as *recover* and *re-cover, coop* and *co-op, overage* and *over-age, reform* and *re-form*.

RESEARCH ESSAYS

Whenever you write a research essay or report, you engage in the research process. The seven-step system described in this section is designed to smooth your progress through this complex process.

R1   Step 1: Defining the Assignment

Your first task in any research essay is to conduct an analysis of the research assignment. A fundamental part of that analysis is defining your audience, purpose, and scope; clarifying the assignment instructions; and determining your research requirements.

R1-a   Audience

The voice you adopt in your essay, the vocabulary you use, and the stance you take will depend on your understanding of your audience and its expectations. Ask yourself the following questions:

- If the audience is specified in the assignment, what are the expectations of that audience and how well informed is it?
- If the audience is not specified, should I seek guidance from my instructor?
- If the audience is my instructor, what are his or her expectations?
- Is the audience likely to have a position on the topic? What is it?
- What response do I want to elicit from my audience?

R1-b   Purpose

Purpose refers to the aim or objective of your essay. Try to determine the common purpose(s) to which the assignment seems to lend itself. Does the topic provide opportunities for you to *describe, inform, recommend, evaluate, argue, interpret,* or some combination of these?

Before you complete the preliminary phase of your research project, you should know the answers to these questions:

- What is the purpose of the assignment? Is the purpose explicitly stated or is it implied?
- Am I being asked to write a demonstration essay, to show I have mastered certain concepts in a specified field?

- Am I invited to define my own approach or is an approach assigned?
- If an argument is called for, are the main terms given?

R1-c Scope

Scope refers to the breadth or range of the assignment. To define the scope of an essay, ask yourself these questions:

- Does the assignment specify the extent or range of the research that will be required?
- Does the assignment specify the length of the essay?
- Are the terms in the assignment general or specific?
- If the terms are general, does the assignment give me the option of defining them more precisely?
- Does the assignment allow me to create my own topic or scope?

R1-d The Instructions

One of the first things you should do when you get a research assignment is analyze the instructions.

The key to assignments is the verbs that indicate the tasks you are being asked to perform. You should underline the verbs in the assignment instructions and, using the following glossary as a guide, specify the demands each verb makes.

- *Account for* asks you to perform causal analysis—that is, use supporting detail to demonstrate how and why a phenomenon occurred.
- *Analyze* means to take something apart to see how it works. In an analysis, you may examine the parts, steps, sections, or causes of your topic (cf. *synthesize*).
- *Assess* requires you to examine a topic critically to determine its value or significance.
- *Compare* asks you to examine two or more topics to find similarities and differences.
- *Contrast* requires you to examine two or more topics to find differences.
- *Defend* asks you to express a position and defend it.
- *Define* requires you to invent your definition by (1) drawing on your research, (2) using the classical defining mechanism of placing your topic in the class to which it belongs and then distinguishing it from all other members of that

119

class, (3) employing an invented definition, or (4) using such definitional techniques as history and background, comparison and contrast, or context. A definitional essay asks you to make definition the focus of your essay.

- *Evaluate* asks you to judge a topic. You cannot evaluate without first creating and announcing the criteria or standards you employ in evaluating your topic. It is up to you to establish and defend the criteria of your evaluation.

- *Review* requires you to present a summary of the topic and examine the summary for the purpose of evaluation.

- *Summarize* asks you to express briefly the main points of the topic.

- *Synthesize* requires you to put parts back together to make a unified whole (cf. *analyze*).

- *Trace* asks you to ascertain the successive stages of an event or phenomenon.

R1-e   Research Requirements

To determine what your research requirements are, you must first decide if you need to use primary sources or if you can complete the assignment using secondary sources alone. Primary sources are an integral part of the topic you are writing about, while secondary sources are interpretations of that topic.

R2   Step 2: Developing a Preliminary Thesis

You can narrow and focus a topic by developing a *preliminary thesis* (also called a *working thesis*). A preliminary thesis has two functions: (1) it names the topic, and (2) it indicates your anticipated position on that topic. One of the easiest ways to arrive at a preliminary thesis is to use the looping technique (see F2-c). The statement you write about can be as simple as *When I think of X, I feel. . . .* Here are three other techniques you can use to narrow and focus a topic:

1. *Limit the time frame.* If the topic encompasses a twenty-year period, change the time frame to a ten-year period unless your instructor objects.

2. *Limit the geographical scope.* Instead of assessing the impact of the most recent recession on Canada as a whole, concentrate your assessment on one region.

3.   *Reduce the number of topic elements.* If your topic has three parts, eliminating one of those parts will make it more manageable. If the topic calls for you to compare and contrast four subjects, reduce the number of subjects to two or three.

R3   Step 3: Conducting Research

Once you are satisfied with your preliminary thesis, you can start creating a *working bibliography*, a list of works you want to consult or research you want to initiate. If you want to do primary research, you will need specific guidance from your instructor. Less challenging is secondary research, which involves building a working bibliography consisting of secondary sources. The place where you will most likely initiate your search for sources is the library.

R3-a   Reference Books

Your library's reference section is the ideal place to begin your search because it contains general works that will help you gain an overview of your topic.

BROWSING EFFICIENTLY

A helpful way to find references is to browse through the appropriate section of your library's stacks.

When you find the area in the stacks containing books related to your subject, your browsing can begin. Check the tables of contents and the indexes of the books for key words related to your topic.

Turn to the back of each book and find out whether the volume includes an annotated bibliography, which comments on the usefulness and relevance of each source it lists.

USING NEW RESOURCES

Many libraries subscribe to computerized databases—specialized electronic listings of books, articles, and essays—that are available in the sciences, humanities, and social sciences. These databases use key words to identify the topic or field of all the books, articles, and essays they list. To use a computer database, you merely enter your list of key words, and the computer conducts the search for you.

Your library may even have the capacity to do a CD-ROM search. Try to keep abreast of all the developments in electronic resources that can assist you in your research.

R3-b   Electronic Catalogues

After checking various resources in your library's reference section, you should be ready to move on to a more specific search activity: consulting the electronic catalogue. An electronic catalogue is a quick and easy way to search a library's holdings. You can search an electronic catalogue by subject, by author, or by title.

R3-c   Research and the Internet

It takes considerable time and practice to become efficient at using the Internet as a research tool, but your task is greatly simplified if you use a search engine that supports Boolean terms. The three primary Boolean terms—AND, OR, and NOT—link topics in order to narrow or expand a search. The Boolean logic associated with each of these terms is described below.

- AND narrows a search by finding only documents containing all of the specified words or phrases. For example, if you search for *cats AND dogs*, only documents containing both words will be retrieved.

- OR expands a search by finding documents containing at least one of the specified words or phrases. For example, if you search for *cats OR dogs*, documents in which either word appears will be retrieved.

- NOT narrows a search by excluding documents containing specified words or phrases. For example, if you search for *cats AND NOT dogs*, all documents containing the word *cats* will be retrieved, except for those documents also containing the word *dogs*. (Note that most search engines will reject your search request if you use the Boolean term NOT alone; preface this term with AND.)

Search engines such as AltaVista not only support Boolean terms but also allow you to search for phrases rather than individual words by putting the words in double quotation marks. Unfortunately, many search engines that support Boolean terms give priority to commercial sites in their retrievals. One search engine that (so far) does not practise such preferential treatment is Google. Google supports the use of quotation marks around words but not Boolean terms.

R3-d   The Working Bibliography

As you conduct your library and Internet searches, you should continue to build a working bibliography consisting of sources that are relevant to your topic and preliminary thesis.

Each book and periodical article citation in your working bibliography should include the following:

BOOK	**ARTICLE**
Call number	Author(s)
Author(s)	Title and subtitle
Title and subtitle	Title of journal, magazine, or newspaper
Edition	Date and page numbers
City of publication	Volume and issue numbers
Publisher's name	
Year of publication	

Before you leave this stage of the research process, answer these questions:

1. Are all the listed sources relevant to my topic?

2. Do the sources cover all facets of my topic?

3. Are my sources current or are they dated?

4. If my topic is a polarizing issue, do my sources reflect both sides of the argument?

5. Is my working bibliography too ambitious? How much time do I have to complete my research essay and what can I accomplish within that time?

R4 Step 4: Reading

Unlike general readers, researchers are concerned with understanding the strengths and weaknesses of their sources. They read in a structured and systematic fashion and engage in the activities of previewing, note-taking, and taking stock.

R4-a Previewing

Begin the reading process by acquiring an overview of the material. If the source is a book, you can ascertain its general content by reading the preface and last chapter or final paragraphs, and by looking at the table of contents and the index. The table of contents in particular will help you ascertain those parts of the book that are most relevant to your topic. For more information about previewing, skimming, and scanning, see F3-a.

R4-b Note-Taking

As you read, take careful, detailed, systematic notes. (For a discussion of note-taking, see R5.) The kinds of notes you take during the reading process will depend on your topic and preliminary thesis; generally, they will include the following:

- ideas and facts that support or contradict your thesis;
- your own questions and comments about the material;
- examples of the author's biases and assumptions;
- any concepts or key terms that are relevant to your topic.

If you plan to read the source more than once, you may wish to refrain from note-taking until the second reading. Just as note-taking during a lecture can interfere with your ability to absorb information, note-taking during a first reading can interfere with your ability to follow an argument or analysis.

R4-c Taking Stock

At the conclusion of your reading and note-taking, compile a list of the research tasks that remain. Ask yourself:

- Do I understand all the key terms relevant to my topic?
- What questions do I need to answer?
- Has my thesis changed as a result of my reading?
- Do I have a good understanding of the strengths and weaknesses of my sources?
- Do I have a good understanding of each author's assumptions or biases?
- Do I have all the sources I need to write about my topic?

R5 Step 5: Using Note Cards

There are various ways to take notes. The most common is to use 3" × 5" index cards.

The first card you prepare for an individual source is the *bibliography card*. On this card write down the same bibliographical information that appears in the source's citation in the working bibliography (see R3-d). (If you are using cards to build a working bibliography and have already created a card for the source, you do not need to create a second card.) The three other cards you create will contain notes that perform the functions of *summarizing, quoting,* and *paraphrasing*.

1. *Summary.* When you summarize a passage, section, or chapter, you produce a brief statement (in your own words) of the main point or points. A summary note should not run longer than two sentences.

2. *Quotation.* When you quote a passage, you copy it word for word and enclose it in quotation marks. If there is a page break in the middle of the passage you are quoting, indicate the break with a slash; the slash will indicate which page you should cite in your parenthetical reference should you later decide to use only part of the quotation.

3. *Paraphrase.* The paraphrase note is the longest note you will create. When you paraphrase a passage, you restate the information or meaning in your own words. Because a paraphrase contains approximately the same number of words as the original passage, you should use this kind of note only when you think that all or most of the information conveyed in the passage will prove useful at some point.

Each of the three types of cards should include the page number(s) of the source from which the note derives. You can experiment with rearranging the cards in various ways to see how the notes might be most effectively ordered in your essay.

COMPUTER *tip*

You can store your notes electronically in computer documents created for that purpose. Computer storage offers two main advantages: (1) if your notes are extensive, you can use your word processor's search feature to locate information quickly; and (2) you can use the cut-and-paste feature to move material from your notes into your research essay.

R6 Step 6: Drafting the Essay

If time permits, you should write an initial draft of your research essay at least two weeks before the due date. Once you have completed your first draft, set it aside for a few days; imposing this distance will allow you to start the revising process with a fresh and critical eye. See the drafting process, F4, and writing an introductory paragraph, C6-a.

R6-a Outlining

There are three main types of outlines: the sentence outline, the topical outline, and the paragraph outline. A *sentence outline* uses sentences to establish a blueprint for the essay. Before constructing a sentence outline, you must know what the major divisions of your essay are going to be.

In a *topical outline*, you list your topics and subtopics using only key words or phrases. A *paragraph outline* uses, as its name implies, paragraphs as its basic outlining tool.

R6-b Segmenting

In this simple technique, also known as *sectioning*, you settle for a general map. You sketch only the major segments of your project. Once you have done this, you assemble your notes under the appropriate segment headings and begin to write.

Segmenting allows you to tackle a manageable element immediately and not be intimidated by the size of your task. After you create your general map and assemble your information under the appropriate headings, you can start writing about whichever segment you want. With a word-processing program, you can easily assemble the segments in their proper order and add any necessary transitional material later.

R6-c Writing a Draft Introduction

Some writers like to tackle the introduction first; others write it last. If you prefer to start with your introduction, don't aim for a polished version at this stage. Writers who try to perfect their introduction before they move on to other drafting tasks often find themselves afflicted with writer's block. Remember that all you need is a base from which to start. You can revise later.

R6-d Incorporating Quotations

SIGNAL PHRASES

Prose quotations of fewer than five typed lines in your essay (MLA style), or of fewer than forty words (APA style), need to be worked skillfully into the text. A quotation that is dropped abruptly into the text will have a jarring effect.

To smooth the transition between text and quotation, you should preface the quotation with a signal phrase. A widely used signal phrase is the phrase *According to* followed by the author's name:

Cultural factors played a major role in Japan's post–1945 economic recovery. According to Kennedy, "There was social ethos in favor of hard work . . ." (417).

NOTE: Signal phrases should be used to introduce paraphrases and summaries as well.

Another common signal phrase uses the following model:

Kennedy points out that "there was social ethos in favor of hard work . . ." (417).

The word *As*, the author's name, and an appropriate verb may also be used:

As Kennedy points out, "There was social ethos in favor of hard work . . ." (417).

If the quotation is not an independent clause but is instead a word, phrase, or dependent clause, you need to weave the quotation into your own sentence.

Kennedy draws a vivid contrast between Japan's tradition of government intervention in the economy and "the American laissez-faire approach" (417).

For information about punctuation with quotations, see P4.

VERBS IN SIGNAL PHRASES

The verb you use in an *Author + verb + that* or an *As + author + verb* signal-phrase construction provides readers with a sense of the source's purpose. For example, *reports* suggests an attempt to inform, while *argues* suggests an attempt to persuade. Following is a list of verbs commonly found in both *Author + verb + that* and *As + author + verb* signal-phrase constructions.

acknowledges	contends	points out
admits	declares	recommends
advises	explains	reflects
argues	implies	remarks
asserts	indicates	says
claims	maintains	states
comments	notes	suggests
confirms	observes	writes

SIGNAL STATEMENTS

If you wish to provide more information than can be accommodated in a signal phrase, you may instead use a signal statement. If the statement is an independent clause, it is separated from the quotation by a colon.

Kennedy identifies the economic challenges Japan faced and the principal factors that enabled it to stage its dramatic post-1945 economic recovery:

> Although badly damaged by the 1937–1945 war, and cut off from its traditional markets and suppliers, it possessed an industrial infrastructure which could be repaired and a talented, well-educated, and socially cohesive population. . . . (416–17) [MLA style]

BRACKETS AND ELLIPSES

You can use square brackets and/or ellipses to make a quotation fit grammatically into your own sentence. An excess of ellipsis dots and brackets in the same passage makes for difficult reading, so use these marks of punctuation sparingly.

When using MLA style, enclose the ellipses within brackets. For further information about brackets and ellipses, see P8 and P10.

R7 Step 7: Revising the Essay

You can make the revising process more manageable if you focus on one facet of your essay at a time. To achieve this focus, make use of the four editing sweeps in F5.

In the proofreading sweep, also check for formatting errors. Specifically, check the following basic format requirements:

- separate title page or necessary information on the first page
- pagination in top right-hand corner of each page except the title page
- indented paragraphs
- aligned left margin
- double-spacing throughout
- correct parenthetic referencing
- correct quotation formats
- correct documentation style in Works Cited, Bibliography, or References list

DOCUMENTATION

Different academic disciplines use different systems of documentation. The Modern Language Association (MLA) style, presented in the *MLA Handbook for Writers of Research Papers*, is widely used throughout the humanities. The American Psychological Association (APA) style, contained in the *Publication Manual of the American Psychological Association*, is widely followed by writers and students in the social sciences. The Council of Biology Editors (CBE) style, presented in *Scientific Style and Format*, is a standard reference for those in the scientific community. (Bibliographical information for the MLA, APA, and CBE titles, and for style manuals used in a variety of disciplines, is provided in Table D-1. The entries in the table reflect the humanities style of documentation presented in *The Chicago Manual of Style*.)

The following examples of book, journal, and newspaper reference entries illustrate the basic differences among MLA, APA, and CBE styles of documentation.

BOOK

Bissoondath, Neil. *Selling Illusions: The Cult of Multiculturalism in Canada.* Toronto: Penguin, 1994. [MLA]

Bissoondath, N. (1994). *Selling illusions: The cult of multiculturalism in Canada.* Toronto: Penguin Books Canada. [APA]

Bissoondath N. 1994. Selling illusions: the cult of multiculturalism in Canada. Toronto: Penguin. 234 p. [CBE]

JOURNAL

Hoben, Allan, and Robert William Hefner. "The Integrative Revolution Revisited." *World Development* 19.1 (1991): 17-30. [MLA]

Hoben, A., & Hefner, R.W. (1991). The integrative revolution revisited. *World Development, 19* (1), 17-30. [APA]

Hoben A, Hefner RW. 1991. The integrative revolution revisited. World Dev 19(1):17-30. [CBE]

NEWSPAPER

Picard, André. "Study Finds 'Gender Gap' in Heart Disease." *Globe and Mail* 1 March 2001: A6. [MLA]

Picard, A. (2001, March 1). Study finds 'gender gap' in heart disease. *The Globe and Mail*, p. A6. [APA]

Picard A. 2001 Mar 1. Study finds 'gender gap' in heart disease. Globe and Mail;Sect A:6. [CBE]

D1 Avoiding Plagiarism

Quotations, paraphrases, summaries, facts, and other kinds of information drawn from sources must be fully documented. Using someone else's ideas or words without giving credit to the author is plagiarism, a form of theft. *Common knowledge*, information so widely known that it appears in numerous sources (e.g., the population of Ontario), need not be documented.

TABLE D-1 Style Manuals: Selected Disciplines

CHEMISTRY

Dodd, Janet S., ed. *The ACS Style Guide: A Manual for Authors and Editors*. 2nd ed. Washington, DC: American Chemical Society, 1998.

GOVERNMENT

Canada. Public Works and Government Services Canada. Translation Bureau. *The Canadian Style: A Guide to Writing and Editing*. 2nd ed. Toronto: Dundurn Press, 1997.

HUMANITIES

Gibaldi, Joseph. *MLA Handbook for Writers of Research Papers*. 5th ed. New York: Modern Language Association of America, 1999.

(continued)

TABLE D-1   Style Manuals: Selected Disciplines (cont.)

HUMANITIES, NATURAL AND SOCIAL SCIENCES

The Chicago Manual of Style. 14th ed. Chicago: University of Chicago Press, 1993.

JOURNALISM

Buckley, Peter, ed. *The Canadian Press Stylebook: A Guide for Writers and Editors*. 11th ed. Toronto: Canadian Press, 1999.

McFarlane, J.A., and Warren Clements, *The Globe and Mail Style Book: A Guide to Language and Usage*. Toronto: McClelland and Stewart, 1998.

LAW

Canadian Guide to Uniform Legal Citation. 4th ed. Toronto, ON: Carswell, 1998.

Yogis, John A., et al. *Legal Writing and Research Manual*. 5th ed. Toronto, ON: Butterworths Canada, 2000.

MEDICINE

Iverson, Cheryl, et al. *American Medical Association of Style: A Guide for Authors and Editors*. 9th ed. Baltimore, MD: Lippincott Williams and Wilkins, 1997.

MUSIC

Holomon, D. Kern, ed. *Writing about Music: A Style Sheet from the Editors of 19th-Century Music*. Berkeley: University of California Press, 1988.

PHYSICS

American Institute of Physics. *AIP Style Manual*. 4th ed. New York: AIP, 1990.

SCIENCE

Council of Biology Editors. *Scientific Style and Format: The CBE Manual for Authors, Editors, and Publishers*. 6th ed. New York: Cambridge University Press, 1994.

SOCIAL SCIENCES

American Psychological Association. *Publication Manual of the American Psychological Association*. 5th ed. Washington, DC: APA, 2001.

D2 MLA Style

D2-a Parenthetical References

In MLA style, a parenthetical reference identifies a source and refers readers to the full citation of the source in the list of works cited. Following are some sample MLA-style parenthetical references.

Author and page (short quotation)

Prose quotations that run no more than four lines in your essay are integrated into the text and enclosed in double quotation marks. The author's name need not appear in the parenthetical reference if it is included in the signal phrase. (For information about signal phrases, see R6-d.)

```
Japan's post-1945 economic renewal was
driven in part by a "national
commitment to vigorous, high-level
standards of universal education"
(Kennedy 417).
```

Author and page (long quotation)

Prose quotations that run more than four lines are set off from the text by indenting ten spaces from the left margin. Block quotations are not enclosed in quotation marks and the citation follows the period concluding the quotation. (See P4-b.)

Author of more than one source

If the list of works cited contains more than one work by the same author, name the title in the parenthetical reference or in the text.

```
(Shields, Larry's Party 160)
```

If the title of the work is long, use a shortened version in the parenthetical reference.

Two or three authors

If the source has two or three authors, include them in the parenthetical reference or name them in the text.

133

More than three authors

If the source has more than three authors, include in the text or parenthetical reference only the name of the first author followed by *et al.* ("and others").

> A recent study found that depression among stroke victims tends to deepen with time (Simpson et al. 45).

Unidentified author

If the name of the author is unknown, either use the source's full title in the text or use the first two or three words of the title in the parenthetical reference.

Corporate author

Place the names of corporate bodies in the parenthetical reference or in the text. (The preferred placement for long names is in the text.) In the parenthetical reference, shorten words that are commonly abbreviated.

Authors with the same last name

If the works-cited list contains works by two or more authors with the same last name, include the first initial in the parenthetical reference.

> (J. Smith 13)   (D. Smith 45-49)

If the initial is shared, write the first name in full.

Multivolume work

If your essay cites more than one volume of a multivolume work, include the volume number in the parenthetical reference. Note that a space separates the colon and the page number.

> In her diary, Virginia Woolf expressed her reservations about <u>Ulysses</u> (2: 199-200).

Indirect quotation

Use the abbreviation *qtd. in* to indicate that you are using someone else's report of a writer's or speaker's words: (qtd. in Kingwell, 14).

D2-b   Content and Bibliographical Notes

MLA allows the use of content and bibliographical notes with parenthetical documentation. These optional elements add to the information provided in the text. *Content notes* offer explanation, comment, or information that would interrupt the flow of the essay if it were included in the text. *Bibliographical notes* either comment on sources or refer readers to sources relevant to the topic under discussion.

Both kinds of notes are formed the same way. Insert a superscript arabic numeral at the appropriate place in the text and then write the note, prefacing it with a matching numeral. Indent the first line of the note like the first line of a paragraph. Position the note either as a footnote at the foot of the page or as an endnote at the end of your essay.

D2-c   List of Works Cited

The list of works cited, which starts on a separate page at the end of the essay, contains complete bibliographical information for all the sources cited in the text. When constructing a works-cited list, follow these guidelines:

- Start the list on a separate page and title the list *Works Cited*.
- Centre the title an inch (2.5 cm) from the top of the page.
- Arrange the list *alphabetically* by the surnames of the authors or editors.
- If a work has no author or editor, alphabetize it according to the first word of its title. If the title's first word is *a*, *an*, or *the*, use the second word to determine placement.
- Do not indent the first line of each entry in the works-cited list. Indent subsequent lines five spaces. This format, called a *hanging indent*, makes the authors' surnames stand out for easy reference. (If your word processor has one, use the hanging-indent feature to format entries.)
- Double-space between the title and the first entry, and between and within entries throughout the list.

For a sample list of works cited, see page 151. Following are some sample works-cited entries.

ITALICS/UNDERLINING AND DASHES

Most word processors allow you to use italics for titles of complete works and special categories of words (see M1). However, the MLA recommends the use of underlining rather than italics on the ground that italicized text is not always as readable as underlined text. If you wish to use italics, the MLA suggests that you obtain your instructor's approval before doing so.

In MLA-style essays, you can use either two hyphens (--) or a word-processing dash (—) to form a dash. There is no space before, between, or after the hyphens.

BOOKS AND OTHER NONPERIODICAL WORKS

One author You will find in a book's title and copyright pages the three basic units of a book entry: (1) author; (2) title; and (3) place of publication, publisher, year of publication. Use a shortened form of the publisher's name (for example, *Scribner's* for *Charles Scribner's Sons, and Oxford UP* for *Oxford University Press*).

> Sakamoto, Kerri. <u>The Electrical Field</u>.
>
> Toronto: Knopf, 1998.

Two or three authors Name the authors according to the order in which they appear on the title page. Invert the name of the first author so that the surname comes first. Separate the authors' names with commas.

> McNaught, Kenneth, and David Bercuson.
>
> <u>The Winnipeg General Strike</u>. Don
>
> Mills, ON: Longman, 1974.

More than three authors Name only the first author listed on the title page, and follow the name with a comma and *et al.* ("and others").

> Betcherman, G., et al. <u>The Canadian
>
> Workplace in Transition</u>. Kingston,
>
> ON: IRC, 1994.

Author with an editor After the author and the title, write the abbreviation *Ed.* ("Edited by") followed by the name of the editor.

> McClelland, Jack. <u>Imagining Canadian
>
> Literature: The Selected Letters of
>
> Jack McClelland</u>. Ed. Sam Solecki.
>
> Toronto: Key Porter, 1998.

Corporate author Begin the entry with the corporate author's name, even if it is the name of the publisher as well.

> Canadian Authors Association. <u>Canadian
> Writer's Guide</u>. Markham, ON:
> Fitzhenry, 1997.

Unidentified author Begin the entry with the title. Recall that titles are alphabetized by the first word other than *a, an,* or *the*.

> <u>The International Guide to English
> Language Programs</u>, 1998. Victoria:
> EI Educ. Intl., 1997.

More than one work by the same author If your works-cited list contains two or more works by the same author, name the author only in the first entry. Begin subsequent entries with three hyphens followed by a period. List the entries alphabetically by title.

> Mistry, Rohinton. <u>A Fine Balance</u>.
> Toronto: McClelland, 1995.

> ---. <u>Such a Long Journey</u>. Toronto:
> McClelland, 1993.

Editor Follow the name or names with the abbreviations *ed.* ("editor") or *eds.* ("editors").

> Heron, Craig, ed. <u>The Workers' Revolt in
> Canada, 1917-1925</u>. Toronto: U of
> Toronto P, 1998.

Translation Begin the entry with the author's name. After the title, write the abbreviation *Trans.* ("Translated by") and follow the abbreviation with the name of the translator.

> Gravel, François. <u>Miss September</u>. Trans.
> Sheila Fischman. Dunvegan, ON:
> Cormorant, 1998.

Edition other than the first If a book's title page indicates a later edition of the book, name the edition, in abbreviated form, after the title in your entry. An edition may be identified by number (*2nd ed.*, *3rd ed.*, etc.), by year (e.g., *2000 ed.*), or by name (*Rev. ed.* for "Revised Edition").

> Siegel, Arthur. <u>Politics and the Media in</u>
>   <u>Canada</u>. 2nd ed. Whitby, ON: McGraw,
>   1996.

Multivolume work If a work has more than one volume, indicate (using the abbreviation *vols.*) the total number of volumes before the publication information.

> Bell, Quentin. <u>Virginia Woolf: A</u>
>   <u>Biography</u>. 2 vols. London: Hogarth,
>   1972.

If your essay cites only one volume, write the volume number before the publication information and the total number of volumes at the end of the entry.

> Bloom, Harold, ed. <u>The Art of the Critic:</u>
>   <u>Literary Theory and Criticism from</u>
>   <u>the Greeks to the Present</u>. Vol. 9.
>   New York: Chelsea, 1989. 11 vols.

Anthology or compilation Follow the name of the editor or compiler with a comma and the abbreviation *ed.* or *comp.*

> Glover, Douglas, ed. <u>Best Canadian</u>
>   <u>Stories 99</u>. Ottawa: Oberon, 1999.

Selection in an anthology or compilation Name the author of the selection, the selection title, and the title of the book. If the book has an editor or compiler, write the abbreviation *Ed.* ("Edited by") or *Comp.* ("Compiled by") after the title, followed by the person's name. Give the inclusive page numbers of the selection after the publication information.

> Klein, A.M. "Haunted House." <u>The</u>
>   <u>Collected Poems of A.M. Klein</u>. Comp.
>   Miriam Waddington. Toronto: McGraw,
>   1974. 22-25.

Cross-references If you are citing two or more selections
from the same collection, create an entry for the collection
and cross-reference individual selections to the entry. For
each selection, write the name of the author and the title,
the last name of the collection's editor, and the inclusive
page numbers.

Di Michele, Mary. "Poem for My Daughter."
        Lecker and David 270-71.

Lecker, Robert, and Jack David, eds. <u>The
        New Canadian Anthology: Poetry and
        Short Fiction in English</u>.
        Scarborough, ON: Nelson, 1988.

Ondaatje, Michael. "King Kong Meets
        Wallace Stevens." Lecker and David
        250-51.

Article in an encyclopedia Name the author of the article (if
there is one), the article's title, the title of the encyclopedia,
any edition number, and the year of publication. (Full publication information is not necessary if the encyclopedia is
well known.) Omit volume and page numbers if the articles
are arranged alphabetically. Follow the same guidelines
when citing an entry in a dictionary.

Doucette, Leonard E. "Drama in French."
        <u>The Canadian Encyclopedia</u>. 2000 ed.

Introduction, preface, foreword, or afterword Name the
author of the element, identify the element, and then give
the title of the book, the author (after the word *By*), and the
editor (if there is one). Capitalize the name of the element
but do not underline it or enclose it in quotation marks. After
the publication information, give the inclusive page numbers
of the element.

Vernon, Lorraine. Afterword. <u>Time
        Capsule: New and Selected Poems</u>. By
        Pat Lowther. Victoria: Polestar,
        1996. 247-51.

Book published before 1900 If the book you are citing was
published before 1900, omit the name of the publisher. Use a
comma, rather than a colon, between the place of publication and the date.

    James, William. The Principles of

            Psychology. New York, 1890.

Pamphlet Treat a pamphlet entry as you would a book entry.

    Leduc, Paul. A Walking Tour of Old

            Montreal. Montreal: City of

            Montreal, 1973.

Government publication If the name of the document's
author is not identified, begin with the name of the government that issued the document, followed by the name of the
government agency.

    Canada. Federal Cultural Policy Review

            Committee. Report of the Federal

            Cultural Policy Review Committee.

            Ottawa: Dept. of Communications,

            Information Services, 1982.

Conference proceedings List conference proceedings as you
would books. After the title, add relevant information about
the conference that is not included in the title.

    King, Karyn, and Rita M. Bean, eds.

            Literary Instruction: Practices,

            Problems, Promises. Proc. of the

            Annual Conf. and Course on Literacy,

            June 1990, U of Pittsburgh.

            Pittsburgh: U of Pittsburgh P, 1990.

Published dissertation List published dissertations as you
would books, but after the title add relevant information. If
the dissertation was published by University Microfilms
International (UMI), include the order number.

    Ames, Barbara. Dreams and Painting: A

            Case Study of the Relationship

```
between an Artist's Dreams and
Paintings. Diss. U of Virginia,
1978. Ann Arbor: UMI, 1979.
7928021.
```

Abstract of a dissertation Give the publication information for the dissertation, followed by the abbreviation *DA* (*Dissertation Abstracts*) or *DAI* (*Dissertation Abstracts International*), the volume number, the date, and the page number. If the *DA* or *DAI* is paginated by the series number *A*, *B*, or *C*, identify the appropriate series number at the end of the page number.

```
Berkman, Anne Elizabeth. "The Quest for
Authenticity: The Novels of Toni
Morrison." Diss. Columbia U, 1988.
DAI 48 (1988): 2059A.
```

ARTICLES AND OTHER PUBLICATIONS IN PERIODICALS

A periodical is a publication, such as a scholarly journal, a magazine, or a newspaper, that appears at regular intervals. When citing a publication in a periodical, follow these general guidelines:

- If an article in a periodical is not printed on consecutive pages, write the first number and a plus sign; for example, to cite the page numbers of an article that appears on pages 34–41 and 78–79, write *34+* (not *34–79*).
- Treat titles of works that appear within titles of articles in quotation marks as you would stand-alone titles: "The Role of Fate in <u>Macbeth</u>" (an article about a play). For information about the treatment of titles of works in general, see M1-a.
- Abbreviate the names of months except for May, June, and July.

Article in a journal paginated by volume For a periodical that numbers pages continuously each year, write the volume number (in arabic numerals) after the journal's title. The issue number and the month or season may be omitted.

```
Woodcock, George. "Managing Hatred in Two
Centuries." Queen's Quarterly 100
(1993): 827-31.
```

Article in a journal paginated by issue

Olson, Gary A. "The Death of Composition
as an Intellectual Discipline."
<u>Composition Studies</u> 28.2 (2000): 33-
41.

Article in a monthly or bimonthly periodical

Kareda, Urjo. "Behind the Scene." <u>Toronto
Life</u> Feb. 2001: 61-66.

Article in a weekly or biweekly periodical

Parks, Tim. "Hell and Back: A New
Translation of Dante's <u>Inferno</u>." <u>New
Yorker</u> 15 Jan. 2001: 84-89.

Article in a daily newspaper List the author (if there is one),
the article's title, the title of the newspaper, the complete
date, and the page number (including the section letter).
Omit any initial article in the newspaper's name (*Vancouver
Sun*, not *The Vancouver Sun*). If an edition is identified on
the masthead, add a comma after the date and name the
edition (e.g., *metro ed.*).

O'Reilly, Finbarr. "<u>Books in Canada</u>
Brought Back to Life by Amazon."
<u>National Post</u> 17 Jan. 2001: B2.

Unidentified author in a periodical

"Freezing the Taxman." <u>Maclean's</u> 21 Mar.
1994: 19.

Editorial or letter in a periodical Add the word *Editorial* or
Letter after the title (if any) or author's name.

"Where's the humanity?" Editorial.
<u>Toronto Star</u> 10 Jan. 2001, metro
ed.: A22.

Review

> Andrew, Sheila. Rev. of <u>The Contexts of
>   Acadian History, 1686-1784</u>, by Naomi
>   E. S. Griffiths. <u>Dalhousie Review</u> 72
>   (1992): 555-57.

OTHER SOURCES

Television or radio program List the episode's title (if any),
the title of the program, the title of the series (if any), the
network, the local station and city (if any), and the broadcast
date. Add other relevant information such as narrator, performers, or director.

> "Episode 5: A Question of Loyalties,
>   1775-1815." <u>Canada: A People's
>   History</u>. CBC-TV. 12 Nov. 2000.

Sound recording Arrange the information in an entry (for
example, composer, performer, conductor) according to your
research emphasis. Include relevant information such as
manufacturer and year of issue. If the recording is not a com-
pact disc, indicate the medium by writing *Audiocassette* or
LP before the manufacturer's name.

> Corigliano, John. <u>The Red Violin</u>. Perf.
>   Joshua Bell. Philharmonia Orchestra.
>   Cond. Esa-Pekka Salonen. Sony
>   Classical, 1998.

Enclose the title of a specific song in quotation marks.

> Krall, Diana. "Devil May Care." By Bob
>   Dorough. <u>When I Look in Your Eyes</u>.
>   Verve, 1999.

Treat a spoken-word recording as you would a musical
recording.

> Thomas, Dylan. "A Child's Christmas in
>   Wales." Read by the author. <u>Dylan
>   Thomas: Volume 1</u>. LP. Caedmon, 1952.

Film or videocassette List the title, the director, the distributor, and the year of release. Other relevant information,
such as the writer, producers, or performers, may be added.

> Just Watch Me: Trudeau and the '70s
>> Generation. Dir. Catherine Annau.
>> Prod. Yves Basaillon and Gerry
>> Flahive. National Film Board, 1999.

If you wish to focus on a particular individual's work on the
production, begin the entry with that person's name,

> Annau, Catherine, dir. Just Watch Me:
>> Trudeau and the '70s Generation.
>> Prod. Yves Basaillon and Gerry
>> Flahive. National Film Board, 1999.

To cite a videocassette, write the word *Videocassette* before
the distributor's name. Include the original release date if relevant.

> Henry V. Dir. Kenneth Branagh. Perf.
>> Kenneth Branagh, Paul Scofield,
>> Derek Jacobi, Ian Holm, and Emma
>> Thompson. 1989. Videocassette.
>> CBS/Fox Video, 1990.

Live performance Begin with the title of the play, concert,
ballet, or opera. Add relevant information, such as director,
conductor, or performers, and conclude the entry with the
location and date of the performance.

> Billy Bishop Goes to War. By John Gray.
>> Dir. and Perf. Eric Peterson and
>> John Gray. Bluma Appel Theatre,
>> Toronto. 24 Sept. 1998.

Work of art State the artist's name, the title of the work, the
name of the organization in which the work is housed, and
the city. If the work is part of a private collection, follow the
title with the name of the individual who owns it.

> Colville, Alex. Hound in Field. National
>> Gallery of Canada, Ottawa.

Map or chart

> <u>Newfoundland and Labrador</u>. Map. St.
>
>> John's: Newfoundland and Labrador
>>
>> Department of Tourism and Culture,
>>
>> 1992.

Interview To cite a published interview or an interview broadcast on television or radio, begin with the name of the person interviewed and the title of the interview. Conclude with the appropriate bibliographical information.

If the interview is untitled or has a title that does not indicate the nature of the source, use the descriptive identifier *Interview*. Add the interviewer's name if known and relevant.

> Shields, Carol. Interview. "More Spice
>
>> Than Nice." <u>Globe and Mail</u> 26 Feb.
>>
>> 2000: D2-3.

Lecture, speech, address, or reading State the speaker's name, the title of the oral presentation, the sponsoring body (if any), and the location and date of the presentation.

> Ignatieff, Michael. "The Rights
>
>> Revolution." The 2000 Massey
>>
>> Lectures. U of Toronto, Convocation
>>
>> Hall, Toronto. 7 Nov. 2000.

If the presentation has no title, write an appropriate description (*Lecture, Address, Reading*, etc.) after the speaker's name.

Personal communication

> Page, P.K. Letter to the author. 16 Apr.
>
>> 1994.

ELECTRONIC SOURCES

Electronic sources include CD-ROMs, e-mail, software programs, Web sites, on-line databases, and information available using telnet, gopher, file transfer protocol (FTP), and other access modes. This section deals specifically with e-mail, CD-ROMs, and Web sources.

145

CAUTION: Be aware that sources on the World Wide Web lack the stability of their print counterparts; an on-line document may be revised or it may even disappear altogether. In addition, there is no guarantee that the information contained in a Web document is of good quality and error-free. For these reasons, you should evaluate Web sources carefully and obtain your instructor's approval before using them in an essay.

Electronic communication To cite electronic mail you have received, begin with the sender's name and, if there is one, the title (taken from the subject line). Then write the phrase *E-mail to the author* followed by the date.

Chiang, Valerie. "Re: Archetypes." E-mail
    to the author. 7 Mar. 2001.

CD-ROM Treat a publication on CD-ROM as you would a book, but indicate the medium (CD-ROM) before the publication information.

The 1999 Canadian Encyclopedia World
    Edition. CD-ROM. Toronto:
    McClelland, 1998.

If you are citing only part of the CD-ROM, state the author of the part and/or the title of the part before the CD-ROM's title.

Vastokas, Joan M. "Native Art." The 1999
    Canadian Encyclopedia World Edition.
    CD-ROM. Toronto: McClelland, 1998.

WEB SOURCES

A citation of an electronic source contains information similar to that found in citations of print sources. When citing a Web source, you must provide information that identifies the source and allows readers to locate it. In MLA style, the electronic address (or URL) of a Web source is enclosed in angle brackets.

<http://www.nelson.com>

NOTE: In MLA style, an URL that must be divided between two lines should be broken only after a slash.

A Web source citation consists of applicable items from the list below. Following the list are sample MLA-style entries for various types of Web sources.

1. Name of the author or site owner, or name of the editor, translator, or compiler followed by the abbreviation *ed.*, *trans.*, or *comp.*

2. Title of a short work within a scholarly project, book, database, or periodical

3. Title of the scholarly project, book, database, or periodical; or, for a professional or personal site with no title, a descriptive identifier such as *Home page*

4. Name of the editor, translator, or compiler of the online book, preceded by the abbreviation *Ed., Trans.,* or *Comp*; or name of the editor of the scholarly project or database

5. Publication information for any print version of the source (relevant publication facts not given in the source may be added in brackets)

6. Version number of the source or, for a journal, identifying information such as the volume and issue numbers

7. Date of the electronic publication or of the latest update

8. Name of any sponsoring body associated with the Web site or, for a journal, the number range or total number of pages or paragraphs (if they are numbered)

9. Access date

10. Electronic address, or URL

Scholarly project

<u>Anthology of Middle English Literature</u>.
Ed. Anniina Jokinen. 5 Sept. 2000.
13 Nov. 2000 <http://
www.luminarium.org/medlit/>.

Document within a scholarly project

Schiller, Friedrich. "The Sport of
Destiny." Trans. Marian Klopfer.
<u>Nineteenth-Century German Stories</u>.
Ed. Robert Godwin-Jones. 1994.

Foreign Lang. Dept., Virginia
Commonwealth U. 12 Jan. 2001
<http://www.vcu.edu/hasweb/for/
schiller/sport_e.html>.

Professional site

Periodical Writers Association of Canada.
Home page. 30 Oct. 2000 <http://
www.web.net/~pwac/welcome.html>.

Book

Montgomery, Lucy Maud. <u>Anne of Green
Gables</u>. [1908.] Project Gutenberg.
14 Nov. 2000 <http://
www.literature.org/authors/
montgomery-lucy-maud/
anne-of-green-gables>.

Article in an information database

"Canadian Literature: 1960 and Beyond."
<u>Encyclopedia Britannica Online</u>. 18
Jan. 2001 <http://search.eb.com/bol/
topic?eu=108739&sctn=3>.

Article in a journal

Ward, Ian. "Shakespeare and the Politics
of Community." <u>Early Modern Literary
Studies</u> 4.3 (1999): 45 pars. 3 Jan.
2001 <http://www.shu.ac.uk/schools/
cs/emls/04-3/wardshak.html>.

Article in a magazine

Bemrose, John. "Finding Reality in
Fiction." <u>Maclean's Online</u>. 17 July
2000. 8 Aug. 2000 <http://

```
www.macleans.ca/xta-asp/
storynav.asp?/2000/07/17/Cover/
37130.shtml>.
```

Article in a newspaper

```
Richler, Mordecai. "Fighting Words." New
     York Times on the Web. 1 June 1997.
     31 Aug. 1999 <http://
     www.nytimes.com/books/97/06/01/
     reviews/970601.01richlet.html>.
```

D2-d MLA-Style Sample Essay

See pages 150 and 151.

Author's name, instructor's name, course's name and section number, and date typed 1" (2.5 cm) from top of first page and flush with left margin

Freda Johnson

Instructor: Jack Finnbogason

English 309, Section S10

27 November 2000

Author's last name and page number typed 1/2" (1.25 cm) from top of each page

Title centred on page

"A Personal, Private Yowl":

Edward Albee and the

Autobiographical Impulse

In the preface to his play

The American Dream, Edward Albee

writes: "Every honest work is a

personal, private yowl, a

statement of one individual's

pleasure or pain" (54).

Surprisingly, critics have largely

ignored Albee's own "personal,

private yowl" in their search for

larger themes in his work.

Paragraphs indented five spaces

Gerry McCarthy, one of the few

critics to recognize the importance

of the personal in Albee's plays,

has focused attention on the ways

in which "Albee's theatre bears the

mark of his upbringing" (5). Albee

was abandoned at birth by his

natural parents and adopted by Reed

and Frances Albee, heirs to a chain

of theatres. "Reed Albee was small

and taciturn; his wife [twenty

years younger] tall, imposing,

Works Cited

Albee, Edward. _The American
    Dream_. The American Dream
    and The Zoo Story: _Two Plays
    by Edward Albee_. 1960-61. New
    York: Signet, 1963. 51-127.

--. _Three Tall Women_. New York:
    Dramatists Play Service,
    1994.

--. _Who's Afraid of Virginia
    Woolf?_ New York: Signet,
    1962.

--. _The Zoo Story_. The American
    Dream _and_ The Zoo Story: _Two
    Plays by Edward Albee_. 1959.
    New York: Signet, 1963. 5-49.

Amacher, Richard E. _Edward Albee_.
    Rev. ed. Boston: Twayne,
    1982.

Hirsch, Foster. _Who's Afraid of
    Edward Albee?_ Berkeley:
    Creative Arts, 1978.

McCarthy, Gerry. _Edward Albee_.
    London: Macmillan, 1987.

Roudané, Matthew C. _Understanding
    Edward Albee_. South Carolina:
    U of South Carolina P, 1987.

Works Cited
typed, centred,
1″ (2.5 cm)
from top of
page

First line flush
left; subsequent
lines indented
five spaces

D3 APA Style

D3-a Parenthetical Citations

In APA style, a parenthetical citation in the text identifies the source and enables readers to locate the source in a list of references at the end of the essay. A typical parenthetical citation includes the author's name and the year of publication. (The inclusion of the date reflects the importance of currency of research in the social sciences.) Page numbers are usually provided only for direct quotations. Following are some sample APA citations.

Author and date

Place a comma between the author and the date in the parenthetical citation. If the author is named in the text, place the date immediately after the name.

> People with Type O blood are more likely
> to develop duodenal ulcers than people
> with Type A, B, or AB blood (Eisenberg,
> 1978).

> Eisenberg (1978) found that people with
> Type O blood are more likely to develop
> duodenal ulcers than people with Type A,
> B, or AB blood.

Author, date, and page (short quotation)

Quotations of fewer than forty words are integrated into the text and enclosed in double quotation marks. Note the use of the past tense (*reported*) in the text and the inclusion of the abbreviation *p.* before the page number in the parenthetical citation.

> As Schulsinger (1992) reported, "The
> greatest workplace stress occurs when
> jobs are high in stressors and low in
> controllability" (p. 56).

If the author's name does not appear in the signal phrase, place it in the parenthetical citation at the end of the quotation.

> According to one report, "The greatest workplace stress occurs when jobs are high in stressors and low in controllability" (Schulsinger, 1978, p. 56).

Author, date, and page (long quotation)

Quotations of more than forty words are set off from the text by indenting five spaces from the left margin. Quotation marks are omitted. The parenthetical citation follows the period at the end of the quotation.

Two authors

If a work has two authors, use both names in all citations. Note the use of the ampersand (&) in the parenthetical citation and the spelled-out *and* in the text.

> The outcome measures used in the study have been criticized (Campbell & Tsuang, 2001).

> Campbell and Tsuang (2001) have criticized the outcome measures used in the study.

Three to five authors

If a work has three to five authors, list all their names in the text or the parenthetical citation the first time you cite the work: (Rosenthal, Kelly, Allen, & Santos, 1995).

In subsequent citations, use only the name of the first author followed by *et al.* ("and others"): Rosenthal et al. (1995) found that ...

Six or more authors

If a work has six or more authors, use only the first author's name followed by *et al.* in all citations, including the first.

Unidentified author

If the author's name is unknown, include in the parenthetical citation the work's title and the year of publication.

Corporate author

Spell out the name of a corporate body in the text.

> The Consensus Development Panel (1982)
> concluded that "the cluster of symptoms
> does not represent a single disease"
> (p. 627).

Authors with the same surname

If your reference list contains works by two or more authors with the same last name, include the first author's initials in all citations.

More than one work in parentheses

Works by different authors who appear in the same parenthetical citation are listed in alphabetical order by the first author's surname and separated by semicolons.

> (Braun, 1991; Langer et al., 1986;
> Wilkinson, 2000)

Two or more works by the same author are arranged by date of publication and separated by commas: (Kamani, 1994, 1999, 2001)

Personal communication

Identify published personal communications, such as letters and memos, in the text rather than in the list of references. Cite the sender's initials and surname, the words *personal communication*, and the date.

> (C. Misaka, personal communication,
> February 26, 2001)

D3-b Content Footnotes

Like the content note in MLA style, a content footnote is an optional element that expands on substantive information in the text. Content footnotes should not be repositories for complex or unnecessary information. The APA recommends that a content footnote convey no more than one idea.

A superscript arabic numeral indicates the content footnote's position in the text. The first line of a footnote is indented like the first line of a paragraph. Footnotes are typed (double-spaced) on a separate page in the order of their appearance in the essay.

D3-c List of References

In APA style, the list of references provides bibliographical information for an essay's parenthetical citations. The reference list, titled *References*, starts on a separate page at the end of the essay. Entries in a reference list are alphabetically arranged by the surnames of the authors or editors. Reference entries that lack authors or editors are alphabetized by the first word of the title, excluding *a, an,* or *the*. Double-spacing is used between and within entries throughout the list.

For individual reference entries, APA uses the hanging-indent style. In this style, the first line of the entry is aligned with the left margin and subsequent lines are indented five spaces.

```
American Psychological Association.

     Publication Manual of the American

     Psychological Association. 5th ed.

     Washington, DC: APA, 2001.
```

Listed below are APA guidelines for creating reference entries, followed by sample entries for various types of sources. For a sample APA reference list, see page 166.

1. Invert authors' names that precede titles; do not invert authors' names that follow titles. Use initials instead of first and middle names in all authors' names. If there is more than one author, list all names (do not use *et al.*), separate the names with commas, and use an ampersand (&).

2. Follow the last author's name with the date of publication (in parentheses). If no date is available, write in its place *n.d.* (in parentheses).

3. Italicize titles and subtitles of books. Capitalize only the first word of the title and any subtitle, along with all proper nouns.

4. Italicize titles and volume numbers of periodicals. Capitalize periodical titles as you would titles of books.

5. Do not enclose titles of articles in quotation marks. Capitalize only the first word of the article's title and any subtitle, along with all proper nouns.

6. Include any initial article in the names of newspapers (*The Globe and Mail*, not *Globe and Mail*).

7. Use the abbreviation *p.* or *pp.* before page numbers of newspaper articles and selections in edited books. Do not use the abbreviation before page numbers in journals, magazines, and newsletters.

8. Omit from the names of publishers words that are not required to identify the publisher (*Wiley*, not *John Wiley & Sons*). However, retain the words *Books* and *Press* and spell out the names of university presses. If the author named at the start of the entry is the publisher too, write the word *Author*, not the author/publisher's name, in the publication-information element.

ITALICS/UNDERLINING AND DASHES

APA recommends underlining in manuscripts intended for publication. In student papers, either underlining or italics is acceptable. In APA-style essays, two hyphens (--) are used to indicate a dash. There is no space before, between, or after the hyphens.

BOOKS AND OTHER NONPERIODICAL WORKS

One author

> Morrison, D. R. (1998). *Aid and ebb tide: A history of CIDA and Canadian development assistance.* Waterloo, ON: Wilfrid Laurier University Press.

Two or more authors

> Stolorow, R., Brandshaft, B., & Atwood, G. (1987). *Psychoanalytic treatment: An intersubjective approach.* Hillsdale, NJ: Analytic Press.

Corporate author

Canadian Association of Social Workers. (1994). *Social work code of ethics.* Ottawa: Author.

Unidentified author

Southern Ontario recreational atlas. (1998). Victoria: Phototype Composing.

Order of two or more works by the same author

Sacks, O. (1983). *Awakenings.* New York: Dutton.

Sacks, O. (1995). *An anthropologist on Mars.* New York: Knopf.

Order, same author with same publication date

Eichler, M. 1988a. *Families in Canada today: Recent changes and their policy consequences.* Toronto: Gage.

Eichler, M. 1988b. *Nonsexist research methods: A practical guide.* Boston: Allen & Unwin.

Editor

Caruth, C. (Ed.). (1995). *Trauma: Explorations in memory.* Baltimore: Johns Hopkins University Press.

Edition other than the first

Hale, S. M. (1995). *Controversies in sociology: A Canadian introduction* (2nd ed.). Toronto: Copp Clark.

Selection in an edited book

Modleski, T. (1986). Feminism and the power of interpretation: Some critical readings. In T. deLauretis (Ed.), *Feminist studies/critical studies* (pp. 121-138). Bloomington: Indiana University Press.

Entry in an encyclopedia or dictionary

Jary, D., & Jary, J. (1991). Ethnomethodology. In *The HarperCollins dictionary of sociology* (pp. 153-154). New York: HarperCollins.

Government publication

Badets, J., & Chu, T. W. L. (1994). *Canada's changing immigrant population* (Catalogue No. 96-311E). Ottawa: Minister of Supply and Services.

Published contribution to a symposium

Wheeler, D. (1991). Creating culturally specific AIDS interventions: An example of the ethnographic approach to program evaluation. In K. J. Jaros & G. C. St. Denis (Eds.), *Proceedings of the 1991 Public Health Social Work Institute* (pp. 36-54). Pittsburgh: University of Pittsburgh.

Dissertation abstracted in *DAI*

Gaar, S. J. (1989). Environmental factors associated with emergent literacy in

deaf and hearing children (Doctoral
dissertation, Boston University,
1989). *Dissertation Abstracts
International, 50,* 18007A.

Pendar, J. E. (1982). Undergraduate
psychology majors: Factors
influencing decisions about college,
curriculum and career. *Dissertation
Abstracts International, 42,* 4370A-
4371A. (University Microfilms No.
82-06, 181)

Unpublished manuscript or dissertation

Wahlsten, D. (1991). *Heredity and the
mind.* Unpublished manuscript,
University of Alberta, Edmonton.

PERIODICALS

Article in a journal paginated by volume

London, K., & Nunez, N. (2000). The
effect of jury deliberations on
jurors' propensity to disregard
inadmissible evidence. *Journal of
Applied Psychology, 85,* 932-937.

Article in a journal paginated by issue

Spigelman, C. (1999). Trying for
democracy: Group decision making in
the portfolio classroom. *Composition
Studies, 27*(2), 23-37.

Article in a magazine

Jasperse, S. (1995, February). Manic-
depressive illness and creativity.
Scientific American, 272, 62-67.

Article in a daily newspaper

Vardy, J. (2001, January 17). Technology creating "IT rage" in workplace. *National Post,* p. C6.

Letter to the editor

Shams, Z. (2001, January 11). Women in Iran [Letter to the editor]. *The Globe and Mail,* p. A12.

Review

Jackson, D. D. (1994, March). [Review of the book *Broadsides from the other orders: A book of bugs].* *Smithsonian, 24,* 132-133.

WEB SOURCES

Book

Gray, H. (1918 edition). *Anatomy of the human body.* Retrieved January 17, 2001, from http://www.bartleby.com/107/

Article in a journal

Charles, S. T., Reynolds, C. A., and Gatz, M. (2001, January). Age-related differences and change in positive and negative affect over 23 years. *Journal of Personality and Social Psychology, 80,* 136-151. Retrieved January 22, 2001, from http://www.apa.org/journals/psp/psp801136.html

Spillman, B. C., & Pezzin, L. E. (2000). Potential and active family

caregivers: Changing networks and
the "sandwich generation." *The
Milbank Quarterly, 78.* Retrieved
January 19, 2001, from http://www
.milbank.org/quarterly/7803feat.html

Journal abstract

Hurtz, G. M., and Donovan, J. J. (2000).
Personality and job performance: The
Big Five revisited [Abstract].
Journal of Applied Psychology, 85,
869–879. Retrieved January 15, 2001,
from http://www.apa.org/journals/apl/
1200ab.html#4

Article in a magazine

Blum, D. (1999, January/February).
Attention deficit. *Mother Jones.*
Retrieved July 16, 1999, from http://
www.motherjones.com/mother_jones/JF99/
attentiondeficit.html

Article in a newspaper

Goode, E. (2001, January 16). Patient
suicide brings therapists lasting
pain. *The New York Times on the Web.*
Retrieved January 21, 2001, from
http://www.nytimes.com/2001/01/16/
health/16SUIC.html?pagewanted=all

Review

Kenneally, C. (2000, August 9). [Review of
the book *The making of intelligence*].
Salon. Retrieved September 14, 2000,
from http://salon.com/books/review/
2000/08/09/richardson/index.html

Entry in an encyclopedia

Differential psychology. *Encyclopedia*
Britannica Online. Retrieved October
31, 2000, from http://members.eb
.com/bol/topic?eu=30910&sctn=1

Independent document (unidentified author)

Electronic reference formats recommended
by the American Psychological
Association. (2001, January 10).
Washington, DC: American
Psychological Association. Retrieved
January 16, 2001, from http://
www.apa.org/journals/webref.html

Database

Statistics Canada. (n.d.). *Crimes by type*
of offence. Retrieved January 22,
2001, from the CANSIM database:
http://www.statcan.ca/english/Pgdb/
State/Justice/legal02.htm

D3-d APA-Style Sample Essay

The three main components of an APA essay are the title page, the text or body of the essay, and the list of references. Your title page should include the following elements:

- a page header consisting of the first two or three words of the title, followed by the page number, in the upper right-hand corner;
- a running head consisting of a short title of the essay, set flush left;
- the full title of the essay, centred; and
- identifying information (author's name, course name and section number, instructor's name, and date), centred.

Start the body of the essay on a separate page and include a running head on all pages of the essay. Begin the reference list on a separate page. (For information about setting up a reference list, see D3-c.) Use double-spacing between all lines in the essay and the reference list.

Your instructor may ask that you prepare an *abstract,* a one-paragraph summary of the contents of your essay. The abstract, which should not exceed 120 words, is placed on a separate page between the title page and the text. Your essay may also include one or more appendixes. Appendixes follow the reference list, with each appendix beginning on a separate page.

On the following pages are excerpts from an APA-style essay.[2] Format specifications are pointed out in the marginal notes.

---

[2] Adapted from an essay by Charles F. Carington-Smith, a student in a psychology class.

Running head (short title) set flush left

FRANCIS GALTON: THE INVESTIGATOR

Page header (first two or three words of title and page number) in upper right-hand corner

Full title, author's name, course name and section number, instructor's name, and date centred on page

The Investigator of Individual

Differences: Francis Galton

Charles F. Caringon-Smith

Psychology 307, Section 10

Professor Kinley

April 10, 2001

The Investigator of Individual
Differences: Francis Galton

Full title,
centred at
top of page

The English scientist Francis
Galton (1822-1911) was among the
most brilliant and innovative of
those great nineteenth-century
figures who contributed to the
development of science and the history
of ideas. As one of Galton's
biographers points out, a list of
subjects to which the scientist can be
said to have added knowledge includes
"travel, the weather, stereoscopic
maps, high-pitched whistles, blood
transfusions, composite photography,
finger prints, number forms, word
association, correlation, twins, the
sterility of heiresses, and various
contrivances and inventions" (cited in
Eysenck, 1958, p. 158). Eysenck argues
that "[Galton] has many claims to be
called the founder of modern
psychology, a title usually bestowed on
a methodical, plodding German called
Wundt, whose contributions were of an
administrative rather than of a
creative nature" (p. 158).

Paragraphs
indented
five spaces

In 1859, Darwin's seminal work *The
Origin of Species* was published. The old

References
typed,
centred, at
top of page

References

Blacker, C. P. (1952). <u>Eugenics: Galton and after.</u> London: Duckworth.

Bloomfield, P. (1957). <u>Uncommon people: A study of England's elite.</u> London: Hamish Hamilton.

Eysenck, H. J. (1958). <u>Sense and nonsense.</u> Harmondsworth, England: Penguin.

Fancher, R. E. (1990). <u>Pioneers of psychology.</u> New York: Norton.

Fisher, R. A. (1930). <u>Genetical theory of natural selection.</u> London: Oxford University Press.

Fluegel, J. C., and West, D. J. (1964). <u>A hundred years of psychology.</u> London: Duckworth.

Forrest, D. W. (1974). <u>Francis Galton: The life and work of a Victorian genius.</u> London: Elek.

Galton, F. (1869). <u>Hereditary genius: An inquiry into its laws and consequences.</u> London: Macmillan.

Galton, F. (1889). <u>Natural inheritance.</u> London: Macmillan.

First-line
indent (or,
alternatively,
hanging indent)
for reference
entries

J

JOB-RELATED WRITING

J1 Business Documents

J1-a Memos

One of the simplest documents you will be asked to write is the inter-office memo, an in-house document directed to a person or group of people in the same organization. The memo enables you to retain a hard copy of your communication to act as a reminder or as proof that you have made a request or voiced an opinion. If you use e-mail to communicate with your colleagues, you must decide whether to make a hard copy of memos you receive and send.

COMPUTER^{tip}

The simplicity and convenience of using an e-mail program encourages spontaneous and informal communication. Indeed, research has shown that we say things in an e-mail we would never say to a person's face. Be wary of this pitfall. In everything you write—including e-mail—use language that is appropriate for your audience.

Memos are sent to ask questions, distribute information, make requests, and transmit good or bad news. They may even be used to persuade someone to do something. However, memos should be brief and to the point.

Many of the better word-processing programs have templates for memos built right into them. You may find that the template has been modified to suit the needs of an individual organization. However, if an organization uses a preprinted memo form, it will look something like the one in Figure J-1.

The memo's subject line introduces the reader to the subject immediately and allows the writer to get right to the point in the body of the memo.

Like a business letter, a memo is brief and to the point. Unlike a business letter, a memo lacks a salutation and a formal close. You should sign your memo, though, either with your initials or, if your organization tends to be informal, with your first name. Your signature goes either at the end of the memo or at the top of the memo at the end of the *From* line.

Direct your correspondence to a specific audience. Be action-oriented. Memos and business letters tend to use *I*, *we*, and *you* more than formal essays or written reports. It is useful to direct your message to a specific reader or set of readers and be reader-oriented. Similarly, in business letters or memos, state what action, if any, you or others will take.

FIGURE J-1 Brief Memo

MEMO

AARDVARK EDUCATIONAL MATERIALS

To: Sally Rendall, Director of Operations
From: James Hong, Purchasing Manager
Date: March 14, 2001
Subject: *Business Communications Handbook for Employees*

The Handbook's publication date has been pushed back to August 1.
Would you like us to place a standing order or, given the delay, would
you prefer to investigate alternative titles?

James

COMPUTER*tip*

If you are using e-mail for communications, consider setting up
a formal block close that includes your name, title or position,
your organization's name, your phone and fax numbers, and
your e-mail address. This block of information, called a *signature block,* functions as the signature at the end of a traditional
memo. Format your e-mail so that the signature block is auto-
matically added to all of your outgoing mail.

J1-b   Formal Letters

Letters, like memos, should be clear and concise. Common
letter types include the following:

- good-news letters   - letters of inquiry
- bad-news letters   - persuasive letters

A letter has distinct parts that give its recipient all the necessary information. The fact that letter styles are predictable in
construction makes it easy for a reader who is familiar with

standard letter styles to find information in a letter. The parts of a letter are separated by at least one blank line and the letter's text or body is usually single-spaced.

The main parts of a formal letter are as follows:

- Letterhead/return address
- Date line
- Inside address
- Salutation
- Subject line
- Body or text
- Complimentary close
- Signature block
- Reference initials
- Enclosure notation
- Copy notation

If you use the letterhead of the organization you work for, the return address for your letter is usually preprinted on the organization's stationery. If you are writing a letter that is not on letterhead, you should place your return address at the top of the page. The placement of the return address, like the placement of other parts of the letter, varies according to the format you use. At present, four letter formats are commonly used. The traditional letter format is gradually being replaced by the simpler and more functional full-block, modified-block, and simplified formats. Each of these formats is associated with one of the two punctuation styles outlined below.

1. *Mixed punctuation*

   - In addresses, punctuation is used between elements in a line (*Toronto, ON*) but not at the end of a line.

   - Salutations end with a colon. (A comma is acceptable in personal letters.)

   - Complimentary closes end with a comma.

2. *Open punctuation*

   - In addresses, punctuation is used between elements in a line (*Toronto, ON*) but not at the end of a line.

   - Neither the salutation nor the complimentary close have end punctuation.

TRADITIONAL FORMAT

The traditional format, shown in Figure J-2, has the following characteristics:

- The *letterhead*, consisting of the organization's name and return address, is centred at the top of the page. If

FIGURE J-2 Traditional-Format Letter, Mixed Punctuation

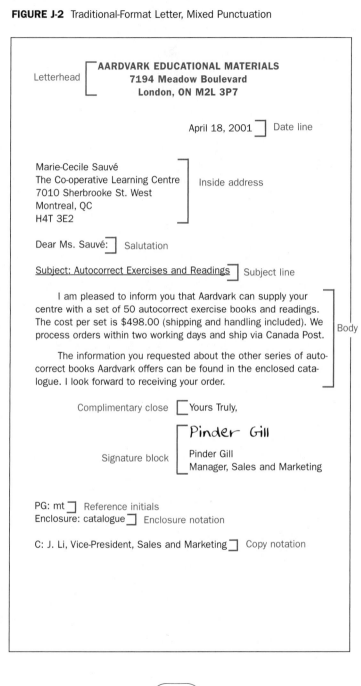

Letterhead **AARDVARK EDUCATIONAL MATERIALS**
7194 Meadow Boulevard
London, ON M2L 3P7

April 18, 2001 Date line

Marie-Cecile Sauvé
The Co-operative Learning Centre
7010 Sherbrooke St. West
Montreal, QC
H4T 3E2 Inside address

Dear Ms. Sauvé: Salutation

Subject: Autocorrect Exercises and Readings Subject line

I am pleased to inform you that Aardvark can supply your centre with a set of 50 autocorrect exercise books and readings. The cost per set is $498.00 (shipping and handling included). We process orders within two working days and ship via Canada Post. Body

The information you requested about the other series of autocorrect books Aardvark offers can be found in the enclosed catalogue. I look forward to receiving your order.

Complimentary close Yours Truly,

Pinder Gill

Signature block Pinder Gill
Manager, Sales and Marketing

PG: mt Reference initials
Enclosure: catalogue Enclosure notation

C: J. Li, Vice-President, Sales and Marketing Copy notation

FIGURE J-3 Placement of Return Address in Traditional-Format Letter

155 Centre St.
Calgary, AB
T2Q 4B2
April 9, 2001

Marie-Cecile Sauvé
The Co-operative Learning Centre
7010 Sherbrooke St. West
Montreal, QC
H4T 3E2

letterhead stationery is not available, a *return address* consisting of the writer's mailing address is placed just to the
right of the centre of the page (see Figure J-3).

- Two to six lines below the letterhead is the *date line*,
  which is placed just to the right of the centre of the page. If
  a return address is used, it is placed immediately above the
  date line.

- The *inside address*, the *salutation*, and the *subject line* are
  flush with the left margin. Each is separated from the element nearest to it by two blank lines. The subject line is
  emphasized by using underlining.

- The first line of each paragraph in the *body* or *text* of the
  letter is indented five spaces. The text is single-spaced with
  one blank line between paragraphs.

- The *complimentary close* appears two lines below the last
  line of text. Like the date line, it is placed to the right of the
  centre of the page.

- Four or five lines below the complimentary close is the *signature block*, which contains the writer's signature, typed
  name, and title. Like the date line and the complimentary
  close, the signature block is placed to the right of the centre
  of the page.

- *Reference initials* (the writer's initials and the typist's initials) are two lines below the last line of the signature block
  and flush with the left margin.

- Immediately below the reference initials is the *enclosure
  notation*.

- Two lines below the enclosure notation is the *copy
  notation*, which lists all individuals (in addition to the
  addressee) receiving the letter.

FIGURE J-4 Simplified-Format Letter, Open Punctuation

AARDVARK EDUCATIONAL MATERIALS
7194 Meadow Boulevard
London, ON M2L 3P7

April 18, 2001

The Co-operative Learning Centre
7010 Sherbrooke St. West
Montreal, QC
H4T 3E2

SUBJECT: AUTOCORRECT EXERCISES AND READINGS

Aardvark Educational Materials offers a full range of autocorrect
exercise books and readings that may meet the educational needs
of your centre. I have taken the liberty of enclosing a catalogue for
your perusal.

If you have any questions about Aardvark's product line, you may
contact me at 519-555-3912. I look forward to hearing from you.

Pinder Gill

Pinder Gill
Manager, Sales and Marketing

PG: mt
Enclosure: catalogue

C: J. Li, Vice-President, Sales and Marketing

FULL-BLOCK FORMAT

The full-block format differs from the traditional format in two
respects: (1) all elements in the letter—except for the letterhead, which is centred at the top of the page—are flush with
the left margin; and (2) the paragraphs in the body of the
letter are not indented.

MODIFIED-BLOCK FORMAT

The modified-block format is the same as the full-block format
except that the date line, complimentary close, and signature
block are placed to the right of the centre of the page (see
Figure J-5).

FIGURE J-5 Good-News Letter Using Modified Block, Mixed Punctuation

---

KALEIDOSCOPE RESEARCH ASSOCIATES
823 STE-CROIX BLVD.
ST. LAURENT, QUEBEC
H4L 3X9

March 14, 2001

Renée Smith
1534 Poplar Street
Prince Albert, SK
S6V 4H2

Dear Ms. Smith:

Subject: Availability of Quebec/Canada Studies Modules

I am very pleased to report that Kaleidoscope Research Associates offers course modules that we believe will meet your stated curriculum needs. I am enclosing overviews of the first five modules in the series for your perusal.

If you require further information, you may reach me at 514-555-7816 during business hours. I look forward to hearing from you.

Yours truly,

Paul Stonjcer

Paul Stonjcer
Sales Manager

PS: hb
Enclosure: Module overviews

FIGURE J-6 Bad-News Letter Using Full-Block Format, Open Punctuation

---

KALEIDOSCOPE RESEARCH ASSOCIATES
823 STE-CROIX BLVD.
ST. LAURENT, QUEBEC
H4L 3X9

March 14, 2001

Renée Smith
1534 Poplar Street
Prince Albert, SK
S6V 4H2

Dear Ms. Smith

Subject: Availability of American Studies Modules

Kaleidoscope Research Associates offers a wide range of modules that are designed for postsecondary courses on various aspects of Canada–U.S. relations.

At present, we do not carry a module that deals specifically with the effects of NAFTA on U.S. ownership in Canada. However, that subject will be addressed in a module Kaleidoscope is currently developing that will investigate NAFTA and its effects on Canada's economy. For more information about this module, please refer to the description in the enclosed catalogue.

As noted in the catalogue, the module's release date is August 17, 2001. You can reserve a copy by filling out the enclosed order form. If you have any further questions about this module, or about other Kaleidoscope modules that address Canada–U.S. relations, you may reach me during business hours at 514-555-7816.

Yours truly

Paul Stonjcer

Paul Stonjcer
Sales Manager

PS: hb
Enclosures: catalogue and order form

SIMPLIFIED FORMAT

The simplified format is the same as the full-block format except that the salutation and the complimentary close are omitted and the subject line appears in capital letters (see Figure J-4). The simplified format is appropriate when you are directing the letter to an organization in general rather than to a specific person in the organization.

SEQUENCING ELEMENTS IN A LETTER

All letters contain a main idea, details, and a close. The order in which you present these different elements depends on the purpose of your letter. If you are conveying *neutral news* or *good news*, you should start with the main idea, follow it up with any supporting details, and end with a positive closing remark (see Figure J-5). If you are conveying *bad news*, start with a neutral comment, explain your position, present the bad news, and end with a positive comment (see Figure J-6). The opening explanatory comment and the concluding positive comment help to offset the negative effects of the bad news.

J1-c   Reports

There are two types of business reports: *formal reports* and *informal reports*. Formal reports are long and comprehensive, and are often circulated outside an organization. Informal reports are less detailed and are usually written for internal circulation only.

FORMAL REPORTS

A formal report contains most or all of the following elements:

1. *Letter of transmittal*. Some formal reports require a letter of transmittal, which introduces the report to readers.

2. *Title page*. The title page includes the title of the report, the name of the organization the report is written for, the date on which the report is submitted, and the names of the author and his or her organization.

3. *Abstract or executive summary*. This critical part of a report highlights the report's most important points, including the author's conclusions or recommendations. An abstract or executive summary should run no longer than one-tenth the length of the report.

4. *Table of contents.* The table of contents lists headers and other major parts of the report, as well as the page number on which each listed element begins.

5. *Problem statement.* The problem statement identifies the problem or issue addressed in the report.

6. *Background.* The background section of the report explains circumstances surrounding the problem. Depending on the nature of the report, you may also use this section to define elements of the analysis, set limits, and review material relevant to the analysis.

7. *Body of the report.* The body of the report is where you present analysis, evaluation, observations, and data relating to the problem.

8. *Conclusion and recommendations.* The conclusion summarizes the main elements of the report and makes recommendations. If your recommendations are extensive, you may format them as items in a list.

9. *Appendix or appendixes.* Appendixes present material that is not an essential part of the body of the report. Tables that support the main text are often presented in this part of a report.

10. *List of figures, tables, and graphs.*

11. *Bibliography.*

12. *Index.* Appropriate only when the report is very long.

Proposal Reports The proposal report, a special type of formal report, seeks to persuade a client of the benefits of following a specified course of action. It may be unsolicited or it may be written in response to a request for a proposal (RPF). Proposal reports contain the following elements:

1. *Introduction.* The introduction identifies the problem and explains why the author's organization is best suited to deal with the problem. The introduction's main purpose is to provide some indication of the validity and cost-effectiveness of the author's proposed solution.

2. *Background.* In this section, the author presents an analysis of the problem.

3. *Plan.* This part sets forth the author's plan for addressing the problem and details the benefits to the

client of implementing the plan. A plan usually includes a preliminary budget and schedule.

4. *Request for approval.* In the final stage of the proposal report, the author asks the client to approve the plan and reminds the client of the plan's main benefits.

INFORMAL REPORTS

Usually three pages or less in length, an informal report has a narrower focus than a formal report. Informal reports may take the form of a memo or letter, or they may be written on an organization's preprinted report form. Here are some common types of informal reports:

analytical report	periodic report
compliance report	progress report
feasibility report	recommendation report
information report	research report
investigative report	situation report (nonrecurring)
justification report	summary report

Most informal reports involve at least one of the following activities:

- checking sources for information
- reviewing records
- making observations
- designing interviews, questionnaires, and surveys
- conducting interviews, questions, and surveys
- doing inventories
- using a library's resources
- conducting electronic searches
- examining government documents

J2 The Job Search

J2-a Cover Letters

Cover letters are letters that accompany a résumé. A cover letter is an exercise in persuasion: your goal is to show the prospective employer that your skills and experience are an excellent match for the job.

Before you draft a cover letter, you should complete a *personal-inventory sheet* organized around such headings as work experience, educational background, occupational goals, and interests and aptitudes. In detailing your occupational goals, you should think about both long- and short-term objectives. Your assessment of your aptitudes should centre on such things as your ability to solve problems, make decisions, handle stress, work independently/cooperatively, show leadership, and be motivated.

COMPUTER *tip*

On-line information about the job search is readily available, and an increasing number of employers are posting career opportunities on the Web. Here are some popular sites:

- CanadianCareers.com (www.canadiancareers.com). This site includes a Canadian job database and offers advice on résumés, cover letters, researching industries and companies, networking, and other job-related topics.

- Career Planning (www.careerplanning.about.com). This American site profiles careers and presents articles on all aspects of career planning.

- Youth Resource Network of Canada (www.youth.gc.ca). This government site provides information about self-assessment and job search techniques, and includes both governmental and nongovernmental job banks.

The following are some suggestions for how you can structure the letter:

- *First paragraph.* The opening paragraph conveys your letter's purpose. If you are responding to an advertisement, refer to it here. Use the first paragraph to establish the reasons for your interest in this particular firm.

- *Second paragraph.* This is the selling paragraph where you demonstrate your suitability for the job. In the second paragraph, you detail your relevant *skills, experience, and education; interests and personal qualities;* and *specific work achievements.* This paragraph should include a reference to the enclosed résumé.

- *Third paragraph.* The third paragraph should establish your expectation of a positive response. Communicate your interest in, and availability for, an interview.

Ideally, your cover letter should be addressed to an appropriate person within the organization. If your letter is directed to the human resources department rather than to a specific person, you should use a subject line in place of a salutation (see Figure J-4). If the letter is written in response to an advertisement that provides a reference or competition number, that number should appear in the subject line.

J2-b   Résumés

A résumé should present relevant information in a clear and concise fashion (see Figure J-7). Résumés contain most or all of the following elements:

- *Name, address, phone number.* This element is centred at the top of the page.
- *Objective (optional).* This element succinctly identifies your current career objective.
- *Indication of availability (optional).* If you are not available to start the job immediately, you should indicate here when you can start.
- *Summary of qualifications (optional).* Some job search experts recommend prefacing the information section of your résumé with a summary of your most relevant qualifications.
- *Education.* You should present your educational history in reverse chronological order. This element should *follow* work experience if it is less relevant to the position.
- *Work experience.* This element, like education, is presented in reverse chronological order.
- *Professional memberships (optional).* Include if relevant.
- *Skills.* This element lists job-related skills. If you were applying for a computer programming position, for example, you would list the different systems and languages you are familiar with.
- *References.* Some experts think that the statement *References are available on request* is sufficient. If you do name your references, you should be confident that they will speak of you in positive terms.

The two most common résumé formats are the chronological format and the functional format. The *chronological format* (shown in Figure J-7) is organized around the Education and Work Experience elements and should be used when you have an established record in both areas. The *functional format,* places more emphasis on your qualifications; job applicants with minimal work experience tend to favour this format.

FIGURE J-7 Chronological Résumé

David Fong
232 5th Avenue
New Westminster, BC V3L 1R4
604-555-9284 (home)
604-555-8567 (work)

OBJECTIVE
To research, master, evaluate, and communicate technologies that contribute to the organization's effectiveness and efficiency.

AVAILABLE
August 15, 2001

EDUCATION

June 1998 to present	**Management Degree in Technology Program** British Columbia Institute of Technology
April 1989 to December 1994	**Business Administration Undergraduate Program** Simon Fraser University
June 1985 to May 1987	**Computer Information Systems Program** Langara College

WORK EXPERIENCE

November 1994 to present	**Senior Technology Planner** Technology Planning Department, ISD Workers' Compensation Board of British Columbia
June 1990 to November 1994	**End-User Analyst 1** Client Services Department, ISD Workers' Compensation Board of British Columbia
September 1988 to June 1990	**Programmer/Analyst 2** Administration, Prevention Division Workers' Compensation Board of British Columbia
January 1986 to May 1986	**Junior Programmer/Analyst (Co-op)** Canada Safeway, Data Processing Centre

(continued)

181

FIGURE J-7 (continued)

CONTINUING EDUCATION

1995–2000   **Gartner Group Symposiums**
Meta Group Infrastructure Architecture
Conference
GIGA Group Summits
Window 2000 Migration Conference
Microsoft Technical Education Conferences
Microsoft Training (MCP Certified—93% Average)

SKILLS
Leadership
- Managed project teams of 3 to 15 members
- Represented WCB at numerous conventions and seminars
- Led emergency, time-boxed DB2 gateway project and served as technology expert on other projects
- Performed a wide range of administrative duties as acting manager

Technical
- Experience with multimedia subject matter
- Preparation of business cases and technical/user manuals
- Web site development
- Analysis of user needs and design of software
- Experience with 3rd and 4th generation programming languages, and Windows NT
- Thin client deployment experience
- Software applications development, testing, and implementation

REFERENCES

Lloyd Bauer
Director, Technology Services
WCB of British Columbia
604-555-7379

Jim Huang
Vice-President and Chief Innovation
Officer
Green Light Dynamics
604-555-1344

Parmit Sandhu
Manager, Technology Planning
WCB of British Columbia
604-555-8408

Elizabeth MacKay
Owner/Manager
MacKay Travel
604-555-0166

J2-c Interviews

The last stage of a job search is the interview. Successful interviewees are people who have thought about the interview process, familiarized themselves with its basic structure, and learned how to stay focused under pressure. They know that an interviewee is judged on presentation as well as content. The person who answers questions clearly, concisely, and confidently leaves a good impression. Although interview techniques vary from one place to another, the following elements often appear.

- An exploration of your background

    In this stage, interviewers probe your education and work experience in more depth.

- Questions in some technical areas

    Interviewers may ask for a detailed response to a simulated problem or ask a few questions that probe your specific knowledge, skills, and experience.

- An exploration of your interpersonal skills and attitudes

    Most employers want to know how well you work with others.

- Inquiries about your career expectations

    The question behind the question here is, "How long can we expect you to work for us?" or "How long will this job satisfy you?"

- A stress test

    An interviewer may check your response to mild stress by challenging something you say. If you are certain of your ground, defend your position politely but firmly. If you are uncertain, review the possible responses and explain your choice. Do not act hostile or uncomfortable.

- Questions about your strengths and weaknesses

    Such questions are standard in an interview. Be balanced in your response, but be sure you identify more strengths than weaknesses. It is probably not a good idea to say you have no weaknesses.

- An opportunity to question the interviewer

  A question usually posed at the end of an interview is "Do you have any questions of us?" Some interviewers see an absence of questions from you as a sign of inadequate preparation for the interview or as a lack of interest in the company or the position. This is an ideal time to show that you have researched the company.

Be aware of what the interviewers will likely ask you and reduce the surprise element, which is the intimidating dimension of an interview. Arrive early, so you aren't in a panic about getting there on time, and also so you can learn a little about the work environment. When you enter the interview room, greet the members of the interview team energetically and confidently. Some experienced interviewees use a notebook as an essential aid; by taking a note or two on a question you are asked, you give yourself time to compose your answer and a reference to check while you answer. Monitor the nonverbal behaviour of your interviewers; if they seem restless, for instance, wind up your answer as quickly as you can. Finally, be sure to do three things at the end of the interview. First, find out when they expect to make their decision. Second, thank them for giving you an interview and stress, one final time, the quality or qualities that make you best suited for the job. Third, mention that you anticipate hearing from them and make your exit.

Once you get home from the interview, it is a good idea to write a brief note to the appropriate person thanking him or her for the interview and stating once again your interest in the job.

J3   Developing Exam Strategies

Use the following lists of strategies as a general guide for all your exam preparations.

J3-a   Before the Exam

1. *Review your study materials.*

   - Review your summary notes from the course.

   - Combine your lecture and summary notes.

- Highlight or underline in your notes key ideas, key concepts, and terms for special study.

- Create a glossary (including definitions) of key terms introduced in the course.

- Select evidence to support each key idea.

- Note the connections among key ideas.

- Use your organized list of key ideas as a study guide.

2. *Preview the exam by reviewing copies of exams from previous years.*

   - Familiarize yourself with the standard format employed.

   - Pay particular attention to the number of questions on the exam and the value of each question.

   - Compare the emphasis given to topics in previous exams with the emphasis your instructor gives to the same topics.

   - Practise answering each of the various types of questions.

   - Discuss the previous exams with your study group.

J3-b During the Exam

1. *Use the first five to ten minutes of the allotted exam time to read, plan, and organize.*

   - Read the instructions before you do anything else.

   - Quickly write down any important facts, definitions, or formulas you think you will need and are afraid you will forget.

   - Decide whether the questions ask for definitions, problem solving, application of knowledge, or explanations. Underline the key words and verbs employed in the questions. (See R1–d.)

   - Develop a strategy for handling the exam in general and each question in particular. If the exam gives you choices, make your choices now. Decide where to start.

- Divide the exam time according to the marks awarded for each question, factoring in the time you allotted to planning and editing.

- Stick to the time you allot yourself for each answer. If you think one answer needs more time, you can always leave some blank space at the end of your answer and come back to that answer later.

- List points for the question you want to answer first and arrange the points in an effective sequence.

- Use the points to develop a thesis or claim (or rephrase the question to formulate a thesis). Remember that your thesis must address the question you are asked.

- Stick to the topic and use specific evidence.

- Remember that each paragraph should relate to your thesis and to the previous paragraph.

- Your conclusion should provide a restatement of the thesis, a summary of the main points, and a comment that synthesizes your argument.

2. *While writing, budget your time and try to write complete, well-organized answers.*

- Use only one side of the exam-book pages and double-space essay and paragraph answers so that you leave yourself room to make additions and corrections when you read over your work.

- Use vocabulary that is appropriate.

- Make use of theories or arguments that are relevant.

- Analyze: don't list or summarize unless the question asks you to do so.

- Make relevant connections between points and explain information clearly.

- Watch the time. If you find you have too much information and not enough time, you will have to edit your argument or use point form.

3. *Use the closing minutes of exam time to revise, edit, and proofread.*

- People who mark exams are primarily interested in the organization and content of your answers.

Remember that a proofreading sweep is not as important as the content, coherence, and logic of your answer.

- Ask yourself these simple editing questions:

  —Have I supported each of my points?

  —Are my facts correct, clearly stated, and relevant?

  —Does each paragraph support and extend my argument? (If a paragraph is irrelevant, delete it.)

J3-c Multiple-Choice and Short-Answer Exams

- Some examiners who use multiple-choice exams subtract the number of wrong answers from the number of right answers. If the exam instructions indicate that this is the case, be cautious about guessing. If you are not confident about your answer, you may be better off leaving a question unanswered.

- On your first pass through an exam, respond only to questions whose answers you are sure of. Later, return to questions you have not answered.

- Be careful with multiple-choice questions that have two or more similar answers. If you are not sure of the answer, come back to the question later.

- Remember that short answers should be unified and to the point.

- Always leave yourself enough time to review.

Index

a/an, 41, 42,142, 155
abbreviations, 103, 111–13, 156
absolute phrases, 44
absolute terms, 91
abstract, 141, 158, 161, 176
acronyms/initialisms, 112
act (event), 6
active voice. *See* voice
adjective clauses, 45, 89
adjectives, 36–38, 43, 91, 96,
    110, 115
adverb clauses, 44–45
adverbs, 36–39, 43–45, 91, 95
afterword, MLA style and, 139
agreement, 62–69
A.M., P.M., 113
analogy paragraph, 18
analysis, 12
    branching and, 5–6
    causal, 10–11
    topic, 2, 6–7, 119
and, subjects and, 62
antecedents, 28, 64, 66–67
    agreement and, 66–67
APA style, 152–66
    articles and, 159–61
    author, date and, 152–54
    authors and, 152–54, 155,
        156–57
    books and, 130, 156–57
    books, parts of, and, 157–58
    content footnotes and,
        154–55
    dash and, 156
    editions and, 157
    editor and, 157
    encyclopedias and, 158
    government publications
        and, 158
    indentation and, 153,
        154–55
    italics and, 156
    journals and, 130, 159–61
    newspapers and, 131, 155
    page citations and, 152–54,
        156, 158–60

    parenthetical references and,
        152–54, 155
    personal communications
        and, 154
    quotation length and,
        99–100, 152–53
    quotations and, 152–53
    reference list and, 155–62,
        166
    review articles and, 161
    underlining and, 156–60
    for volumes, 155, 159–60
    Web sources and, 160–62
apostrophe, 102–3
    nouns and, 26
    possessive case and, 82,
        102–3
appositive phrases, 44, 55
appositives, 44, 55, 86
    colon and, 97–98
    pronouns and, 86
articles, 41–42
    APA style and, 160–61
    definite/indefinite (*See a/an;*
        the)
    in encyclopedias, 139, 158
    MLA style and, 139, 141–42
as if, clauses and, 36
as or *than,* pronouns with, 87
as though, clauses and, 36
audience
    assignments and, 2, 118
    business writing and, 169
    e-mail and, 168–69
    language levels and, 74–76
auxiliary/helping verbs, 32–33

biographical notes, 135
bibliography. *See also* documen-
    tation
    MLA-style notes and, 135
    note cards and, 124–25
    reports and, 178
    research and, 9, 120, 121–22
    working, 121, 122–23
Boolean terms, 122

brackets, 104–5. *See also* parentheses
  angle, 146
brainstorming, 4
branching, 5
browsing, 121

capital letters, 109–11
  APA style and, 155
  hyphens and, 115
cards, note, 124–25
case
  objective, 53, 86
  possessive, 26, 28, 82, 86, 102–3
  pronouns and, 28, 86–88
  subjective, 53, 86
causal analysis, 10–11
Chicago Manual of Style, The, 130
Christensen, Francis, 20–22
citations, 124
claim. *See also* thesis; topic
  positioning main, 23, 24
classification/division
  paragraphs and, 18
clause(s), 43, 44–45
  adjective, 45, 89
  adverb, 45
  combining, 53–55
  defined, 43
  dependent (*See* dependent clauses)
  independent (*See* independent clauses)
  noun, 45–46
  predicates and, 43
  relative, 45
  restrictive/nonrestrictive, 89
  sentences and, 51–52
  subordinate (*See* dependent clauses)
clichés, 75–76
coherence, 16
collective nouns. *See* nouns, collective
colon, 97–98, 101, 105, 134
commands. *See* imperative sentences
comma(s), 94–97, 105
  appositive phrases and, 44

complex sentences and, 52
compound sentences and, 52
coordinating conjunction and, 61
numbers and, 114
parenthetical expressions and, 95–96, 105
quotation marks and, 101
to separate, 94
series and, 94, 96
to set off, 94–97
speaker tags and quotations, 99
comma splice, 60–61
common knowledge, 131
communications, personal, 145, 154. *See also* letters, formal
comparatives, 37, 91
  absolute terms and, 91
comparison
  contrast and, 18
  topics and, 2
complement(s), 30, 43, 45, 50, 64
conjunctions, 40
  coordinating, 40, 49, 52, 54, 94, 96
  correlative, 40, 49
  subordinating, 40, 45, 58
conjunctive adverb, 61
connotation, 74
content footnotes, 154–55
content notes, 135
contractions, 82, 102–3
coordinate adjectives, 38
critical thinking skills, 10–12
cross-references, 9, 139
cumulative adjectives, 38, 96

dash
  APA style and, 105, 156
  hyphen and, 105, 135–36, 156
  MLA style and, 105, 135–36
definition paragraph, 18
denotation, 74
dependent clauses, 43, 45–46, 52, 54, 64
description, 17
development, paragraph, 17–18
development sweep, 13–14

Index

diction, 74–79. *See also* words
dictionaries, 79
direct object, 49–50
direct speech, 99
documentation. *See* APA, MLA
drafting, 2, 11, 12–13, 125–28

editing, 11, 128, 186–87
electronic sources, 121–22,
    145–46, 160–62
ellipses, 105–6, 128
e-mail, 145–46, 168–69
emphasis, 55–56, 105
    italics and, 109
examinations, 184–87
exclamation marks, 42, 97
    quotation marks and, 101
explanation paragraph, 18
expressions, transitional, 18–19,
    95

figures. *See* numbers
footnote numbers, 135, 154–55
    quotation marks and, 102
footnotes. *See* APA style; MLA
    style
freewriting, 4

gender, 68, 89–90
gerund phrases, 43
gerunds, 34–35, 64, 88
Google search engine, 122
government publications, 140,
    158

he/she, 90
highlighting, 8–9, 13–14
homographs, 81
homonyms, 81
homophones, 81–82
hyphen(s), 115–16, 136, 156
    dash and, 105, 136, 156
    solidus or, 103

ideas, sequencing, 16
idioms, 76–77. *See also* phrasal
    verbs
illustration paragraph, 17
imperative mood, 35
imperative sentences, 48, 53, 59
indentation

APA style and, 153, 154–55
    block quotation and, 99–100,
        133
    MLA style and, 135
independent clauses, 43, 44–45,
    58
    combining, 53–55
    complex sentences and, 52
    compound-complex sen-
        tences and, 52
    compound sentences and, 52
    run-on sentences and, 60–61
    semicolon and, 97
    simple sentences and, 51–52
    subordinating conjunctions
        and, 40
indicative mood, 35
indirect object, 49–51
inference, 10
infinitive phrases, 44
infinitives, 34–35, 38, 87, 91–92
initialisms. *See* acronyms/
    initialisms
interjections, 42, 96
Internet. *See* sources, electronic
interruptions, dash and, 105
interviews, 145, 183–84
I or *me,* 86
italics, 101, 108–9, 135–36, 156.
        See also underlining

jargon, 76
job searching, 178–84

language
    ethnicity/race and, 89
    formal/informal, 74–75
    inclusive, 89–90
    plain (*See* euphemisms;
        idioms; jargon)
    sexist, 89–90
    specialized (*See* jargon)
letters (characters)
    capital (*See* capital letters)
    italics and, 109
    lowercase, 109–11
    missing, and apostrophe, 103
    plurals of, 102, 103
    in series, 104
    as words, 109
letters (correspondence)

action-oriented, 169
cover, 178–80
to the editor, 142, 160
formal, 169–76 (*See also*
    communications, personal)
personal, 145
of transmittal, 176
libraries, 121–23
listening skills, 10
looping, 4–5, 120

magazines. *See* articles
marginal notes, 9
measurement
    agreement and, 65
    symbols and units of, 115
memos, 168–69
me or *I,* 86
mind-mapping, 4–5
MLA style, 133–51
    anthologies and, 138–39
    art, works of, and, 144
    authors and, 133–34, 135,
        136–37
    bibliographical notes and,
        135
    books, parts of, and, 138
    books and, 130, 133, 134,
        140
    citations, pages and, 133–34,
        141–43
    citations and, 131–34
    compilations and, 138
    conference proceedings and,
        140
    content notes and, 135
    dash and, 105
    date and, 141–43
    dissertations and, 140–41
    editor and, 136, 137, 138,
        139
    electronic sources and,
        145–46
    ellipses and, 105–6
    encyclopedias and, 139
    film, sound, videotape
        recordings and, 144
    foreword and, 139
    government publications
        and, 140
    indentation and, 135

interviews and, 145
introduction and, 139
italics and, 108
journals and, 130–31,
    141–43
lectures, speeches, readings
    and, 145
maps and charts and, 145
newspapers and, 131, 142
notes and, 135
original/indirect sources and,
    134
pamphlets and, 140
parenthetical references and,
    133–34
performance, live, and, 144
personal communications
    and, 145
preface and, 139
quotation length and, 133
quotations, direct/indirect,
    134
quoted titles and, 141
radio/television programs
    and, 143
review articles and, 143
songs and, 143
spacing and, 135
translation and, 137
for volumes, 138, 141
Web sources and, 145–49
works cited and, 135–49,
    151
modal auxiliary verbs, 33
modes, developmental, 17–18
modifiers, 70–71
    dangling, 70–71
mood, 36
more and *most,* 91

names, 110–12
narration, 17
n.d., 155
nonrestrictive appositive, 44
nonrestrictive/restrictive. *See*
    restrictive/nonrestrictive
nor, agreement and, 62–63
note cards, 124–25
notes. *See also under* APA style;
    MLA style
note-taking, 9, 124

noun clauses, 45–46
nouns, 26–28
    articles and, 41–42
    collective, 27, 63–64
    compound possessive, 102
    count/noncount, 27–28, 64
    gender and, 68
    kinds of, 26
    plural, and singular meaning, 26, 63–64
    plural possessive, 102
    proper, 26, 110–11
    subjects and, 48–49
numbers, 113–15
    page (See page citations)
    parentheses and, 104
    plural, and apostrophe, 102–3
    superscript, 135, 154–56
    as words, 109, 113–14

object complement, 50–51
objective case, 28, 53, 86
object(s), 49–51
    preposition and, 43
    as subjects, 71
    verbs and, 50–51
outline, 2, 3–4, 126

page citations, 125
    APA style and, 152–54
    MLA style and, 133–34
    quotation marks and, 102
paragraph(s), 16–24
    concluding, 24
    defined, 16
    development, 17–18
    introductory, 23
    sequencing ideas and, 16
    special, 14
    special-purpose, 23–24
    structure, 20–22
parallel structure, 18, 20, 56
    faulty, 71–72
paraphrasing, 124–25, 131
parentheses, 104. See also brackets
    acronyms/initialisms and, 112
    emphasis and, 105
    lists and, 104
    sentences in, 109–10

parenthetical references, MLA style and, 133–34
participal phrases, 43
participles
    as adjectives, 34, 38
    with pronouns, 88
    and verbal phrases, 43
    as verbals, 34
particles, phrasal verbs and, 78–79
parts of speech, 26–42
passive voice. See voice
pentad, the, 5–6
period, 101, 112
periodicals. See journals
personal pronouns, 28
phrasal verbs, 78–79
phrase(s), 43–44, 65, 109, 133
    Boolean searches and, 122
place, prepositions and, 77
plagiarism, 131
plurals, 26, 27, 65, 103
possessive case, 86
    apostrophe and, 26, 82, 102–3
    pronouns and, 28
postal abbreviations, 112
    comma and, 94
predicate(s), 49, 58. See also verbs
    clauses and, 43
    combining, 54
    sentences and, 51
prepositional phrases, 43
prepositions, 41, 43, 77
preview, 23
previewing, 8, 123
prewriting, 2–12
process paragraph, 18
pronouns, 28–30
    agreement and, 66–68
    antecedents and, 28, 66–68
    as appositives, 86
    case and, 28, 86–88
    choice of, 88–89
    collective nouns and, 27
    demonstrative, 29
    gender and, 68
    with gerunds, 88
    indefinite, 29–30, 63, 67, 102

with infinitives, 87
intensive, 29
interrogative, 29
with *as* or *than,* 87
with present participles, 88
reciprocal, 30
reflexive, 29
relative, 29, 45, 64
singular/plural, 66–67
as subject complements, 88
subjects and, 48, 63
unclear references and,
    68–69
proofreading, 80, 186–87
    sweep, 13–14, 74, 128
publisher's name, 156
punctuation. *See also various
    punctuation marks*

question marks, 97, 101–2
questions, analysis and, 6–7
quotation marks, 99–102, 122,
    126–27
quotations. *See also* APA style;
    MLA style
    block, 99–100, 133–34, 153
    brackets and, 104–5
    essays and, 126–28
    incorporating, 126–28
    indirect, 99
    length and APA style, 99,
        126, 152–53
    length and MLA style, 99,
        133
    within quotations, 99
    research and, 125, 131
    in sentences, 65–66
    signal phrases and, 126–27
    speaker tags and, 99

reading skills, 7–9
redundancy, 74, 111
references, 121–23. *See also*
    agreement
    APA style and, 155–62
    cross-, 139
    MLA style and, 135–49, 151
    page (*See* page citations)
References, 155–62
relative clauses. *See* adjective
    clauses

repetition, 18, 20
reports, 2, 176–78
research, 3, 121–23. *See also*
    documentation
    assignments (*See* assign-
        ments; essays)
    bibliographies and, 121
    organizing, 118–20
    references and, 11
    restrictive/nonrestrictive, 95
    appositives, 44
    clauses, 88–89
    comma and, 44, 95, 96
résumés, 178, 180–82
revising, 2, 13–14

sacred books, 108
search, job. *See* job searching
search engines, 122
semicolon, 61, 97
    quotation marks and, 101
sentence patterns, 51–53
sentence(s), 16, 44–45
    clauses, 44–45
    complex, 52
    compound, 52
    compound-complex, 52
    construction of, 58–61
    declarative, 53
    defined, 48
    fragments, 58–60
    fused, 60–61
    imperative, 53, 59
    interrogative, 53
    length of, 55–56
    loose, 56
    parts of, 48–50
    periodic, 56
    run-on, 60–61
    simple, 50–52
serial comma, 94
sexism. *See* language, sexist
she/he, 89–90
signal phrases, 126–27, 133,
    153
signal statements, 127–28
skill development, 7–12
skimming and scanning, 8, 123
slash. *See* solidus
solidus, 103–4, 125
    hyphen or, 104

speaker tags, 99, 110
speech
    direct, 99
    parts of, 26–42, 79
spell checkers, 83
spelling, 79–83
split infinitive. *See* infinitives,
    split
stance, 3
    freewriting/looping and, 4
structure
    coordinate, 21–22
    paragraph, 21–22
    parallel, 20, 55–56, 71–72
    sentence, 50–51
    subordinate, 21–22
structure sweep, 13
style manuals, 130, 131–32
subject complement, 30, 50, 64,
    88
subjective case, 28, 53, 86
subject(s), 48, 50–51, 58
    with *and,* 62
    agreement and, 62–65
    collective nouns as, 63–64
    combining, 54
    complements, 50, 64
    compound, 62
    imperative sentences and, 59
    indefinite pronouns as, 63
    missing, 59
    with *or/nor,* 62–63
    verbs and, 50–51, 62–65
subject–verb agreement, 62–65
subjunctive mood, 36
summary, 11, 125
superlatives, 37–38, 91
    absolute terms and, 91
supplementary information,
        parentheses and, 104

techniques
    examination-writing, 184–87
    focusing/narrowing, 120–21
    interview, 183–84
    prewriting, 4–7
tense, 30–32
    agreement and, 65–66
    auxiliary verbs and, 32–33
terms
    absolute, 91

biological, 109
Boolean, 122
explanatory, 95–96
italics for, 101
paired, and hyphen, 116
paired, and solidus, 103
quotation marks and, 101
words as, 101
than or *as,* pronouns with, 87
that
    clauses and, 36, 64
    or which, 89
the, 41–42
    alphabetizing and, 135, 155,
    newspapers' names and, 131,
        142, 156
there, 48, 64
thesis, 16–17, 23–24. *See also*
        claim; dissertations; topic
    developing a, 120–21
    evaluation thesis, 12
    examinations and, 186
title page, 176
titles
    abbreviation of, 111–12, 133
    agreement and, 65
    alphabetizing of, 135, 155
    capital letters and, 111
    comma and, 94
    documentation of (*See* documentation)
    italics and, 108
    lowercase letters and, 111
    with names, 111–12
    quotation marks and, 100–1
    quoted in titles, 141
    of sacred works, 108
tone, 3
    shifts in, 105
topic, 2–7, 118–20, 120–21. *See
        also* claim; thesis
    analysis of, 2, 6–7, 12,
        120–21
    brainstorming and, 4
    branching and, 5
    comparison/contrast and, 18
    freewriting/looping and, 4–5
    head levels and, 3
    introduction and, 23
    mind-mapping and, 4
    outline of, 3, 126

the pentad and, 5–6
purpose and, 118–19
topic sentence, 16, 20–21
transitional expressions, 18–19,
95
transitions, paragraphs and,
18–20, 23
translation
MLA style and, 137

underlining, 108–9. *See also*
italics
APA style and, 156
MLA style and, 135–36
titles, 100–1
unity, 16
URLs. *See* Web sources
us or *we,* 87

verbal phrases, 43–44
fragments and, 60
verbals, 34–35, 38
verbs, 30–36. *See also* predi-
cate(s)
agreement and, 62–65
auxiliary/helping, 32–33
collective nouns and, 62–64
and gerunds, 34–35
and infinitives, 34–35
intransitive, 30, 50
irregular, 33
linking, 30, 50
missing, 59
mood and, 35–36
phrasal, 78–79
principal parts of, 30
in signal phrases, 127
subjects and, 50–51
tenses and, 30, 31–32, 62
transitive, 51
as verbals, 43–44
voice and, 35

voice
active/passive, 35, 71, 118
writer's, 3, 118

Web sources, 146–49, 160–62
we or *us,* 87
which, dependent clauses and,
64
which or *that,* 89
who, dependent clauses and, 64
who, what, when, where, how,
and *why,* 5–6
who or *whom,* 88–89
wordiness. *See* sentence(s),
wordy
word processing, 83, 108
words. *See also* diction
abstract vs. concrete, 75
coined, 101
compound, 115–16
connotation/denotation of, 74
foreign, 109
general vs. specific, 75, 79
as homophones, 81–82
language levels and, 74–75
meaning of, 74
missing, and ellipses, 105–6
plural, and apostrophe, 103
as terms, 101
usage of, 79 (*See also* diction)
as words, 103, 109
working bibliography, 121,
122–23
World Wide Web. *See* Web
sources
writer's stance, 3
writing process, 3–14

yes and *no,* comma with, 96
you, understood, 48

Focus on ESL

ESL students typically encounter certain problems in English grammar and usage, so here to help those students is a table of contents for the sections in this book—the ESL Tips—that deal with those problems.

Count and Noncount Nouns 27
Helping Verbs 32
Verbs and Gerunds 34
Infinitives and Participles as Adjectives 38
Placement of Adverbs 39
Articles and Nouns 42
Missing Subjects and Verbs 59
Verbal-Phrase Fragments 60
Noncount Nouns and Gerunds 64
Gender and Agreement 68
Preposition Used to Indicate Time and Place 77
Phrasal Verbs 78
Homophones: Possession and Contraction 82

CORRECTION ABBREVIATIONS

agr	faulty agreement between verb and subject (G2-a) or between pronoun and antecedent (G2-c)		joined with no punctuation or connecting word (G1-b)
amb	ambiguous pronoun references (G3-a) or phrasing	gen	weak generalization or unnecessarily general statement
awk	awkward construction or phrasing	id	unidiomatic expression: faulty word combination (a common problem with prepositions)
chop	too many short, simple sentences in succession; subordination required (S5-b)	jarg	inappropriate use of technical language; wordy, inflated writing (W1-f)
coh	lack of coherence: sentence, paragraph, or essay is not consistent in structure, logic, and thought (C4)	log	error or weakness in logic; statement does not follow from what precedes it
cs	comma splice: independent clauses joined with only a comma (G1-b)	mixed	mixed construction; sentence contains elements that do not grammatically fit together
dev	weak paragraph structure or development (C3)	mm	misplaced modifier; modifies wrong word (G3-b)
dm	dangling modifier: a modifier with no word in the sentence for it to modify (G3-c)	nsw	no such word exists
doc	missing source or faulty documentation of source	obs	obscure meaning (W1-g)
emph	weak, absent, or inappropriate emphasis (S5-c)	p	error in punctuation (P)
evid	missing or weak evidence or support for statement	¶	faulty paragraph division: new paragraph needed or not needed
form	faulty manuscript form or essay format	//sm	faulty parallelism, or parallelism required (C4-c, G3-d)
frag	sentence fragment: group of words that does not qualify as a sentence (G1-a)	pres	faulty presentation of quotation, paraphrase, summary, or other source material
fs	fused sentence: independent clauses	red	redundant wording (W1-a)

ref	faulty pronoun reference: vague, ambiguous, or misleading (G3-a)
rpt	unnecessary repetition (W1-a)
shift	confusing or unnecessary shift in subject, person, number, tense, voice, or mood
slang	inappropriate use of slang (W1-c)
sp	misspelled word (W3-c)
sub	subordination required (S5-a)
syn	faulty syntax: incorrect word order
t	error in verb tense (B1-c, G2-b)
thesis	absent, weak, or poorly defined and articulated thesis statement in essay (C6-a, R2)
tr	transposed letters
trans	missing, faulty, or weak transition (C4)
?	unclear
unity	paragraph or sequence of paragraphs lack unity
v	incorrect verb form (B1-c)
var	lack of variety in sentence patterns (S5)
w	wordy (W1-a)
wc	inappropriate word choice (W1)
wm	word(s) missing

A Canadian Writer's Pocket Guide contains essential information for writing at school or work. A concise, easy-to-use reference, the book contains all the basics of grammar and style. This handy pocket guide also features guidance and strategies for planning, writing, and revising.

Features
- Up-to-date APA and MLA documentation guidelines
- Canadian usage and style
- New two-colour interior and design
- ESL tips
- Strategies for success at school and on the job

New Web Site
Find terrific resources for grammar review, the writing process, and more!

www.canadianwriterspocketguide2e.nelson.com

Nelson is part of the Thomson Learning family of companies—dedicated to providing innovative approaches to lifelong learning.

Visit Nelson online at: **www.nelson.com**

For your learning solutions:
www.thomsonlearning.com

ISBN 0-17-616973-3

9 780176 169732